LITTLE BOOK OF NIGHTMARES

1

ADULT COLOURING PAGES
BY SAMANTHA READ

Ordering information:
Quantity sales. Special discounts may be available on quantity purchases by corporations, associations, and others at the sole discretion of Samantha Read. For details, contact the publisher at the e-mail address above.

Printed worldwide, on demand.

First printing, 2016

-HISTORY-

The story of how this colouring book came into existence is an interesting one...

When I shop for a colouring book, sometimes it is hard as fuck to find something that I want to colour. Don't get me wrong, I absolutely love every single colouring book that I look at. They inspire me to be a better artist; not only from an illustrators point of view, but also from the view of the colourer. I started thinking, I would love to see more creep, more gore, more horror and I would love to colour it; not just once but over and over in different ways.

I created this book for others like myself who also may want, or need, to colour something freaky-deaky every now and then. Maybe there are others looking for a book filled with monsters and tentacles and all manner of ill creatures that they would never want to meet in the dark. The pieces that made it into this book are a collection of some of the creepiest, weirdest and downright strangest pieces of art that have come from my dark imagination over the past 15 years.

And so I have created this book not just for me, but for you. For the expert who loves to colour all the fine details of the 'Entrails' and for the novice who loves all things 'Zombie' and 'Skulls'. There is no right or wrong way to colour any picture. Just do what you feel.

Thank you in advance for purchasing this book and for helping to fund the next collection as I am hoping to release a few of these creepy colouring books. Don't forget to share with your equally brave and horror-loving friends that may enjoy colouring something different. Something to break away from the norm but that is equally as relaxing and therapeutic.

If you would like to see more, if you have a suggestion for the next book, or to share a coloured page you can find me on:
Instagram: samanthareadva
Twitter: readthisva
Facebook: facebook.com/samanthareadva

-DISCLAIMER-

Some of the art compiled here is the stuff of nightmares. Literally. Some of the image were drawn as interpretations of experiences that friends have shared with me, and some are my own. Be warned, proceed with caution and remember to close the book when you are finished. After all, you never know... Just teasing. In all seriousness, some of this art is not appropriate for the younger ones. Use your discretion with little ones under 13 or so. Just remember is it freaky from cover to cover.

-SPECIAL THANKS-

To Tiffany for all of your hard work with post production; teaching me how and doing when I had a hard time. Also to Sarah and Meg, for your encouragement and help in making this little dream of mine a reality. Finally, to musical genius' Yolandi and Ninja of Die Antwoord and Mr. Rob Zombie; for being the soundtrack to this awesome experience.

THIS BOOK OF NIGHTMARES BELONGS TO

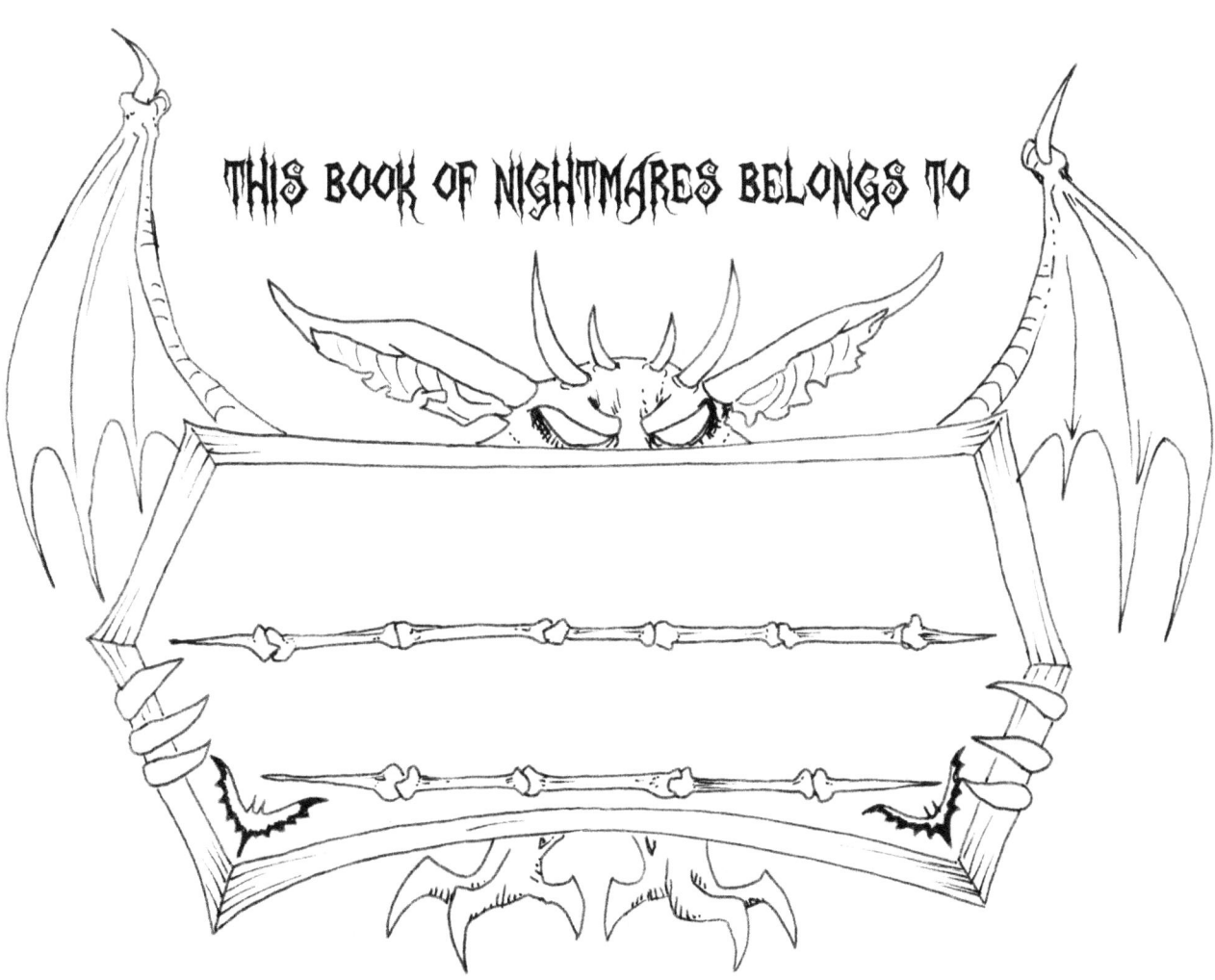

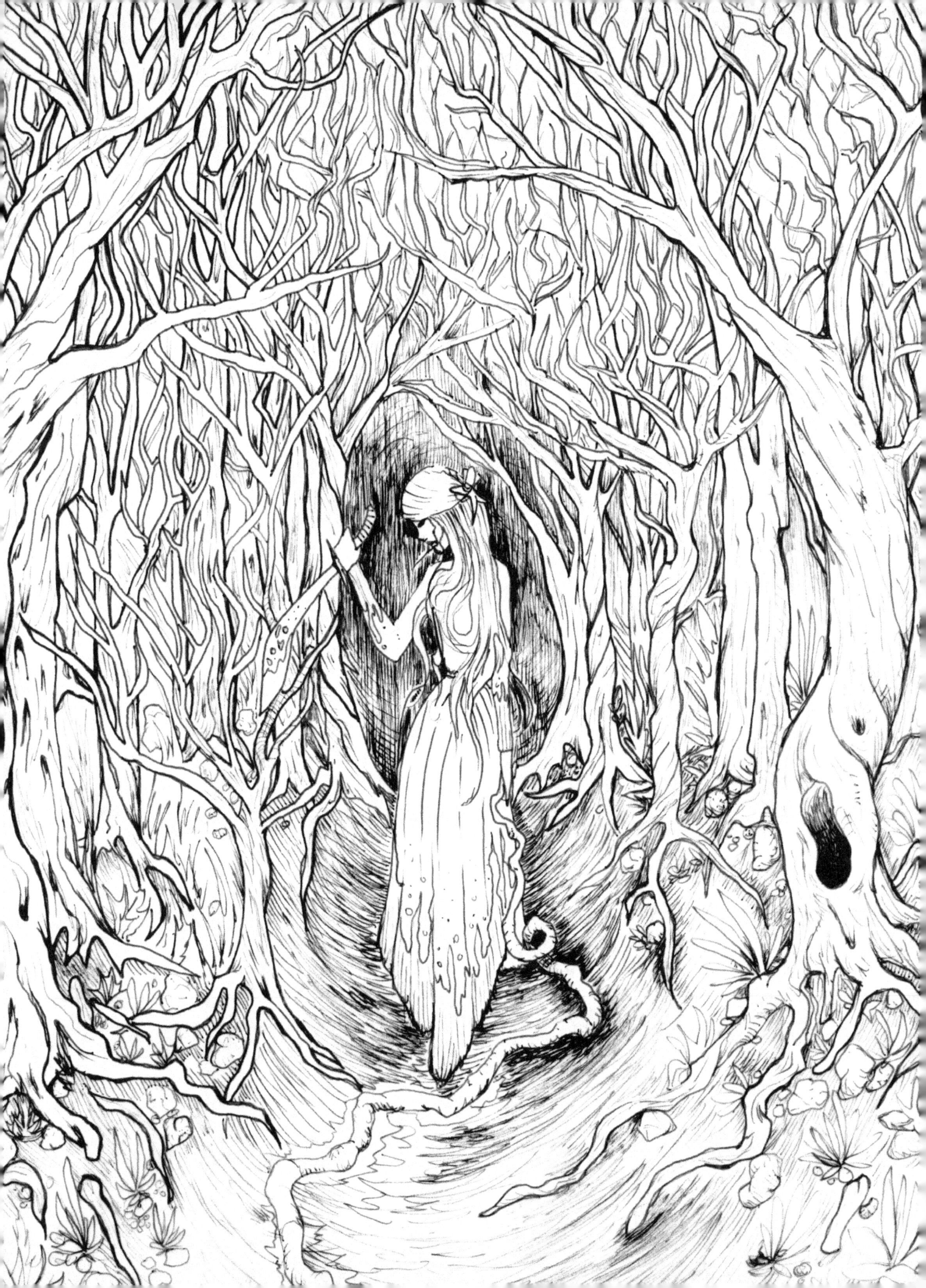

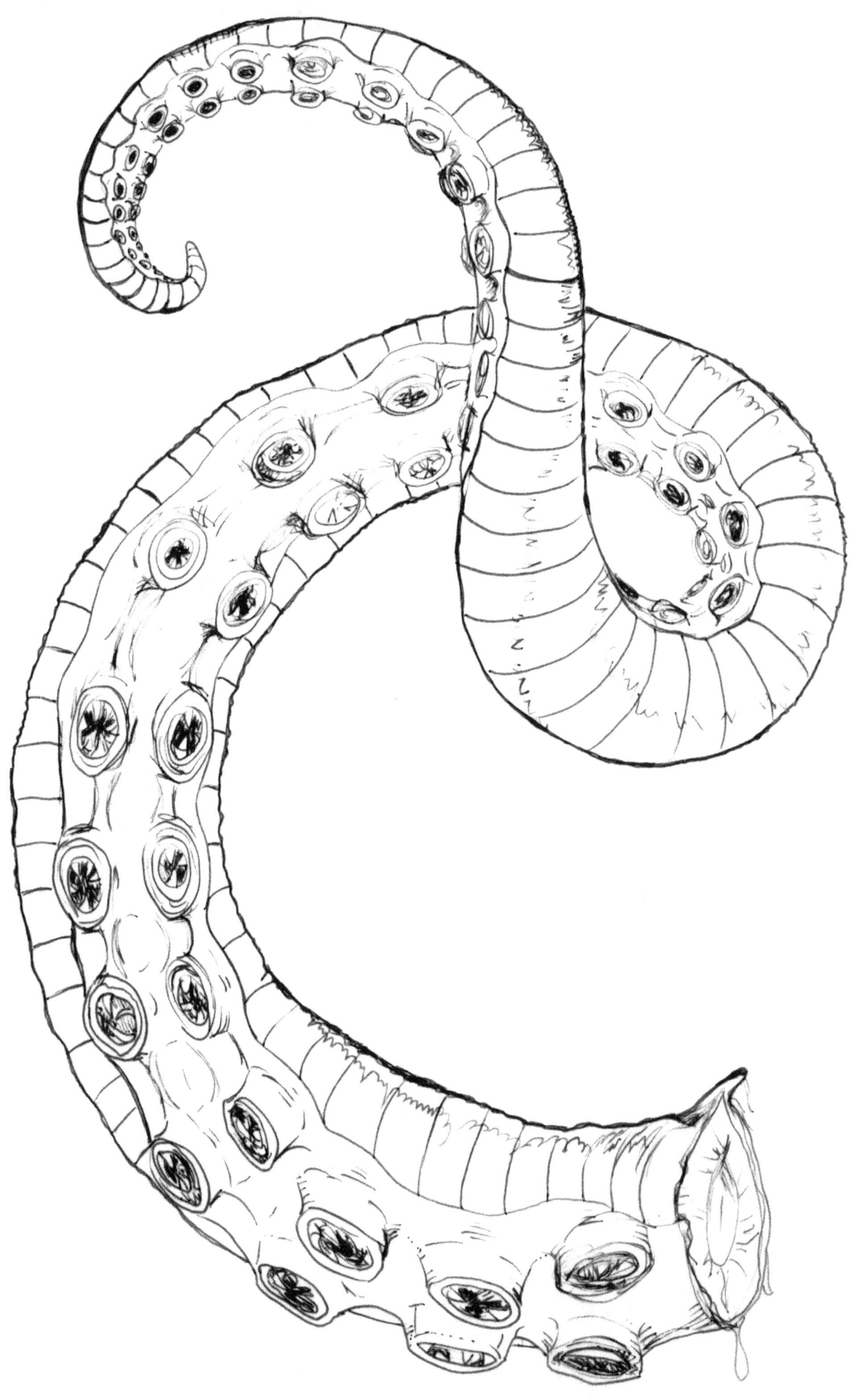

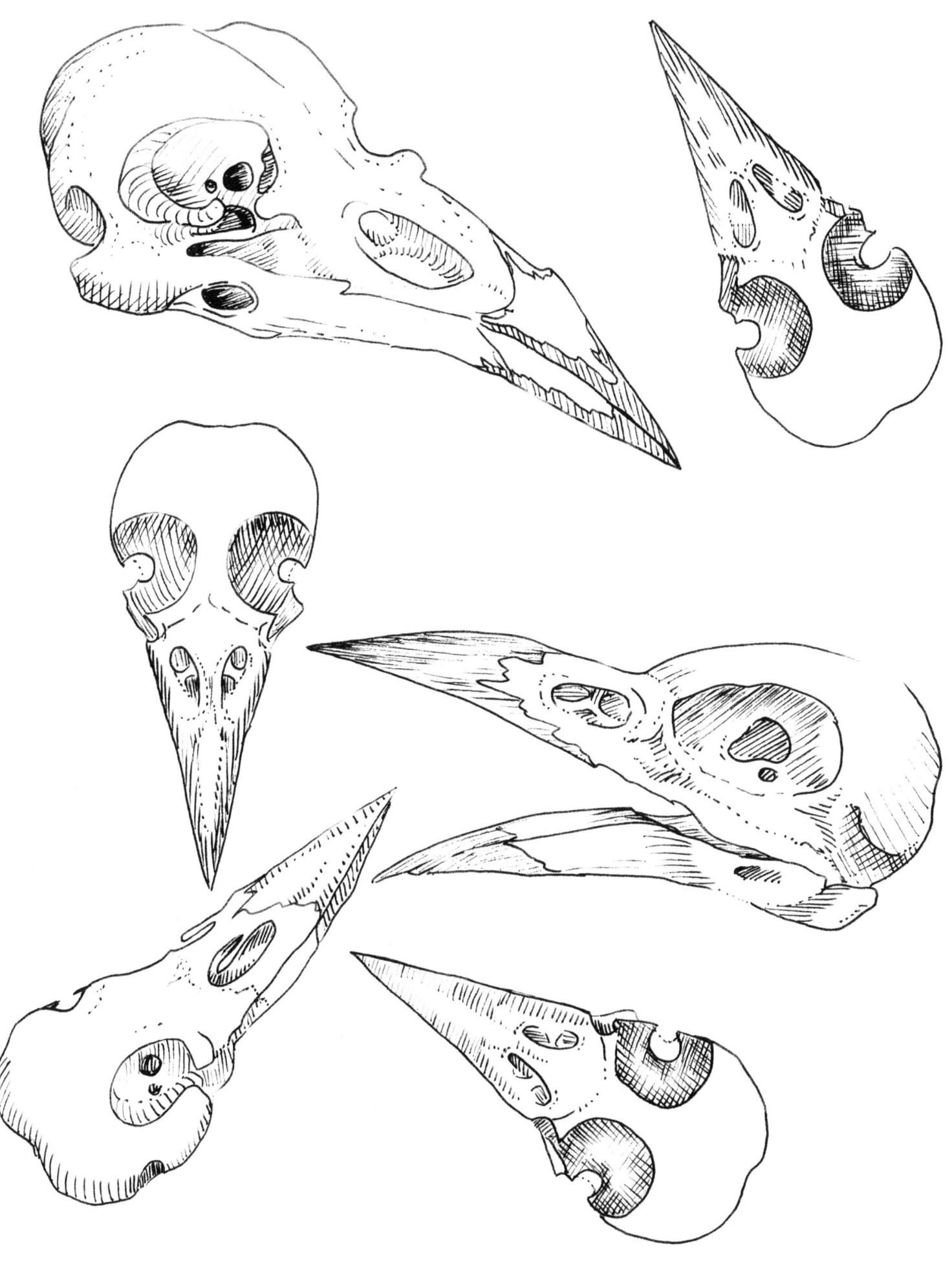

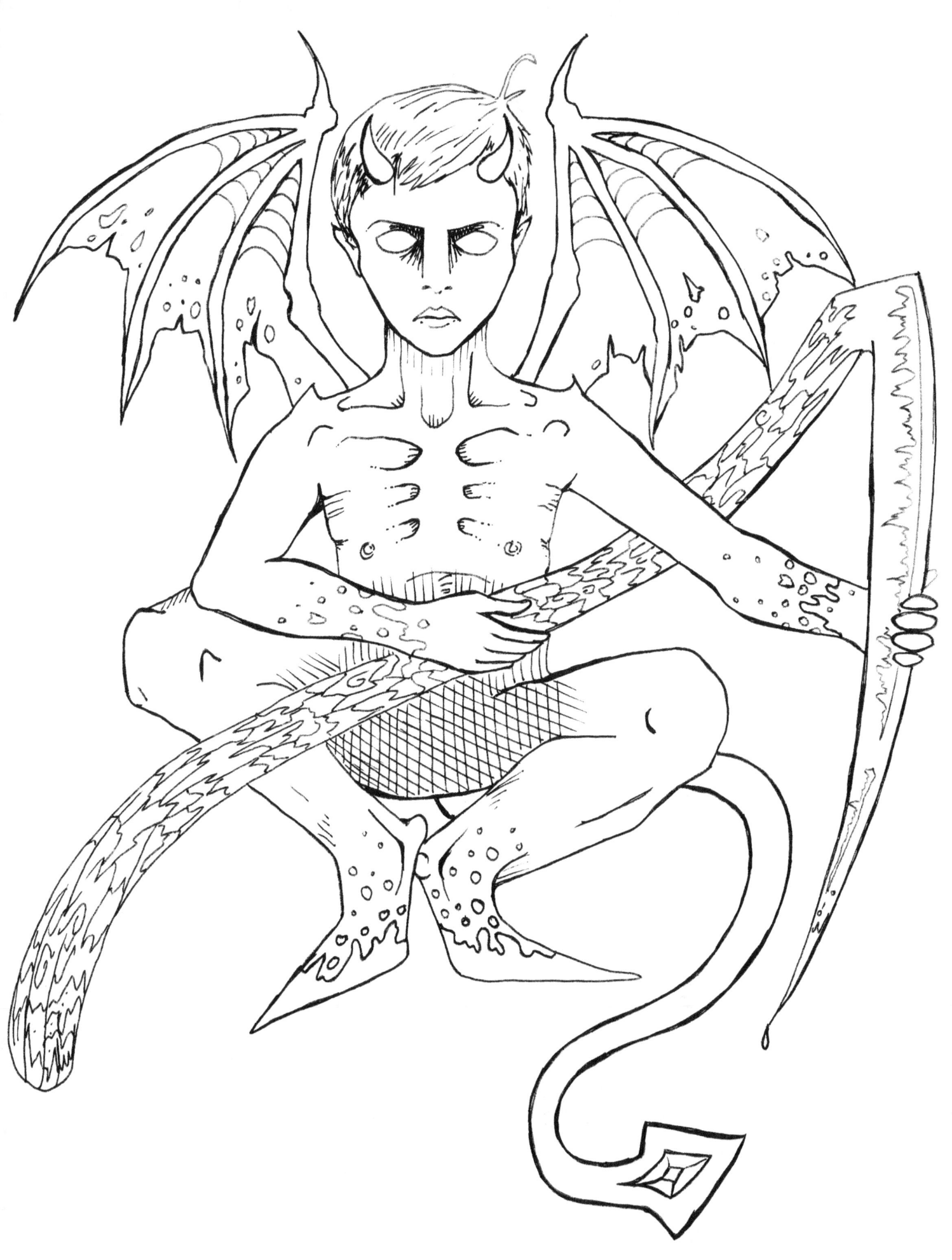

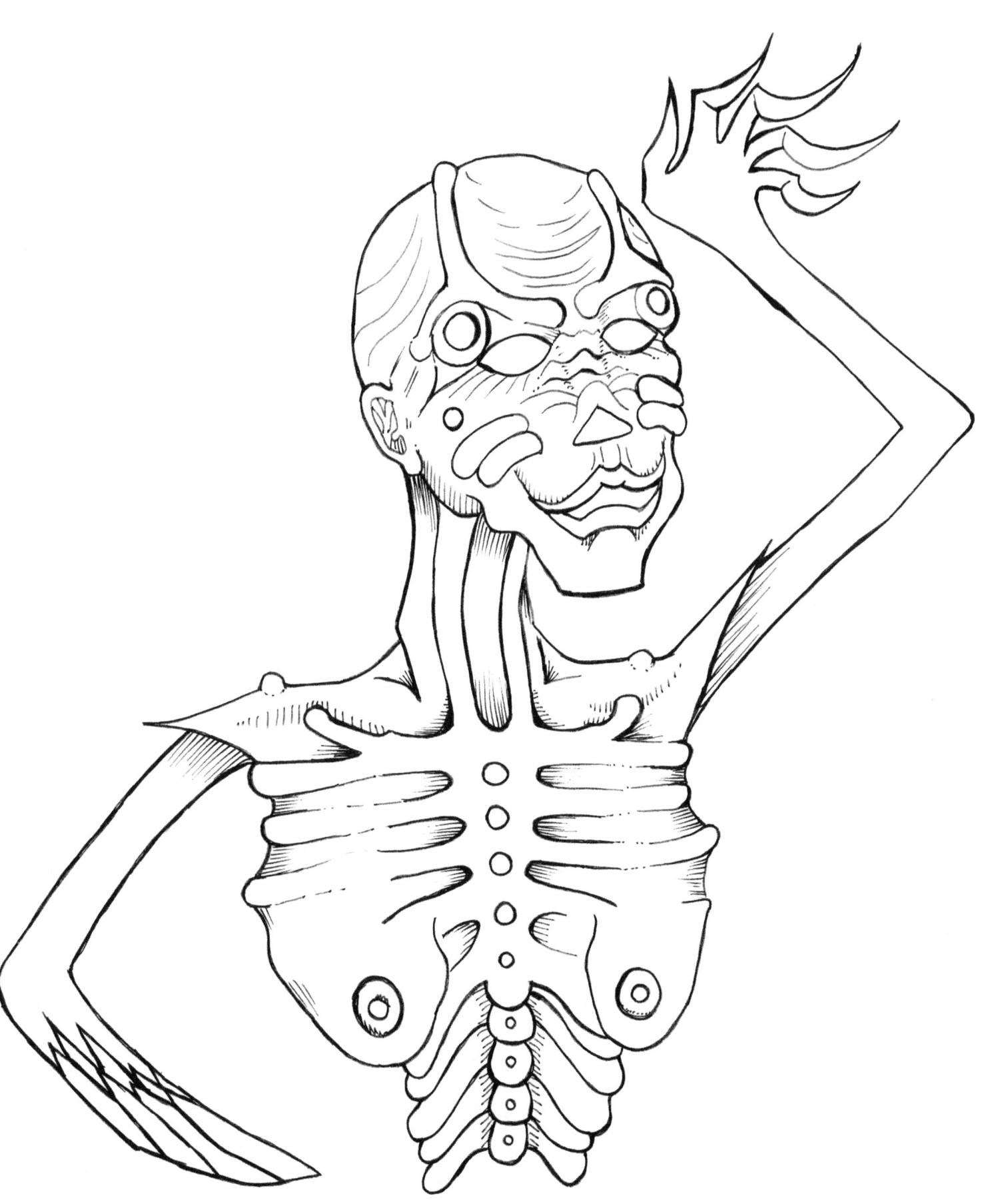

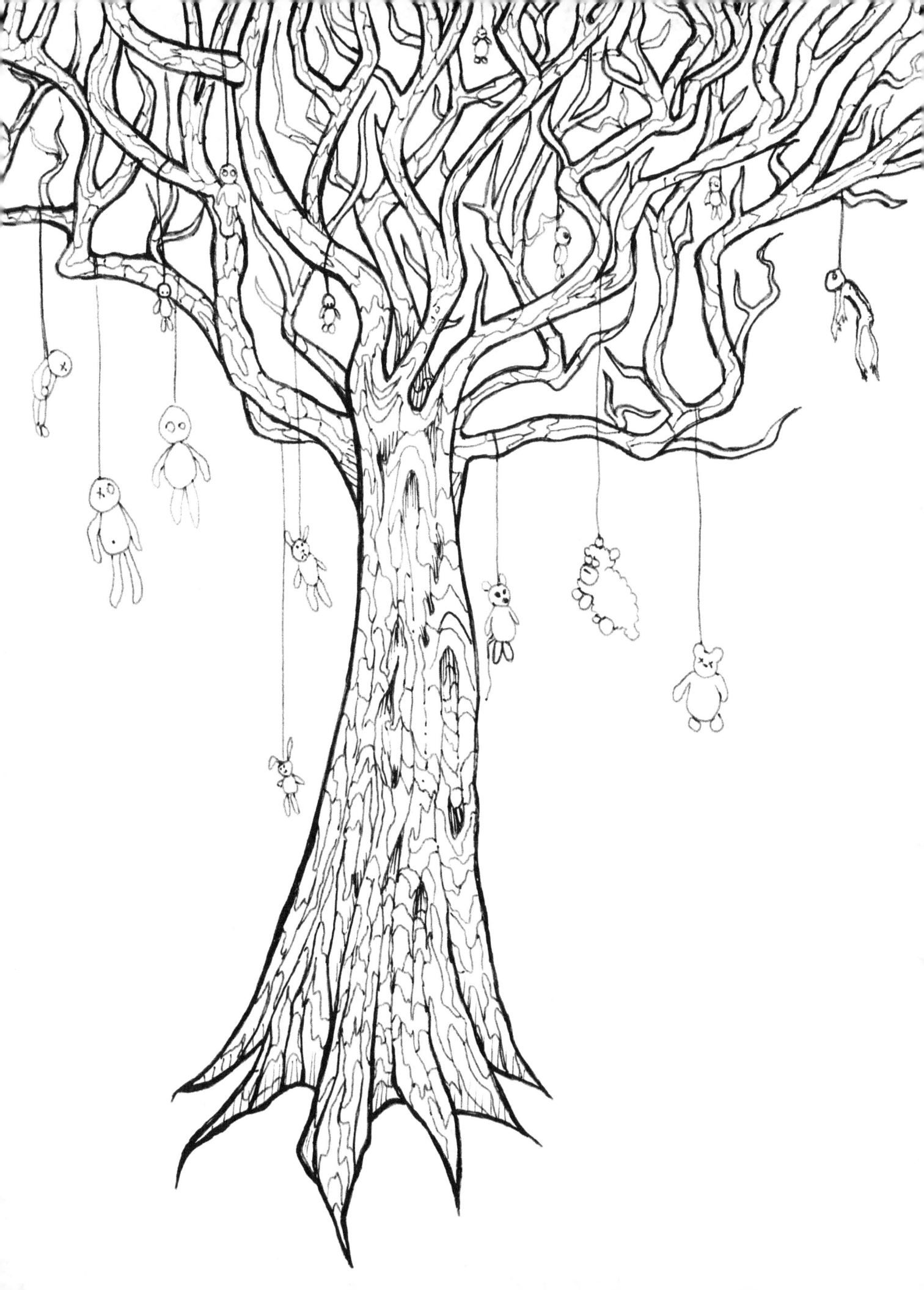

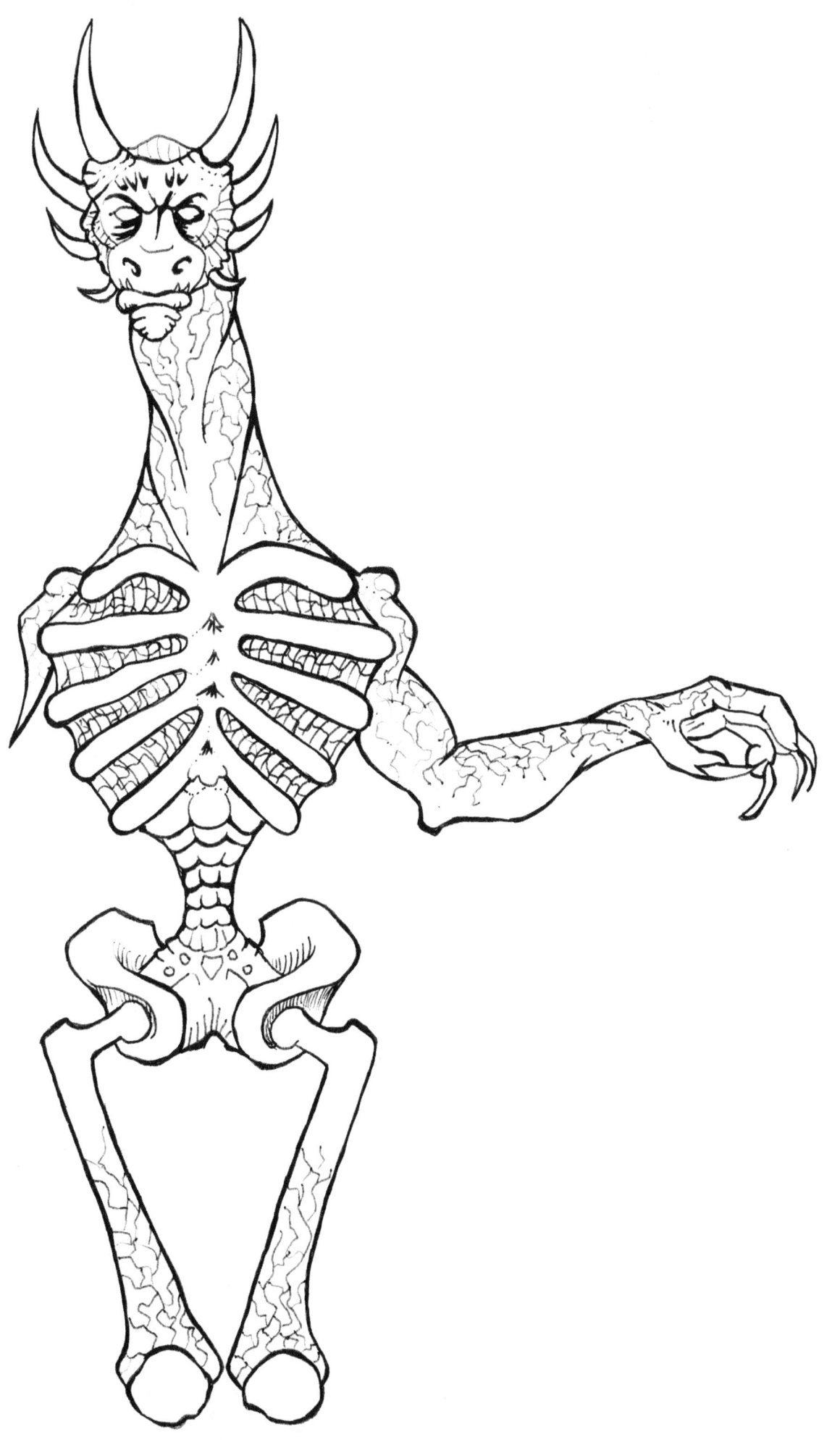

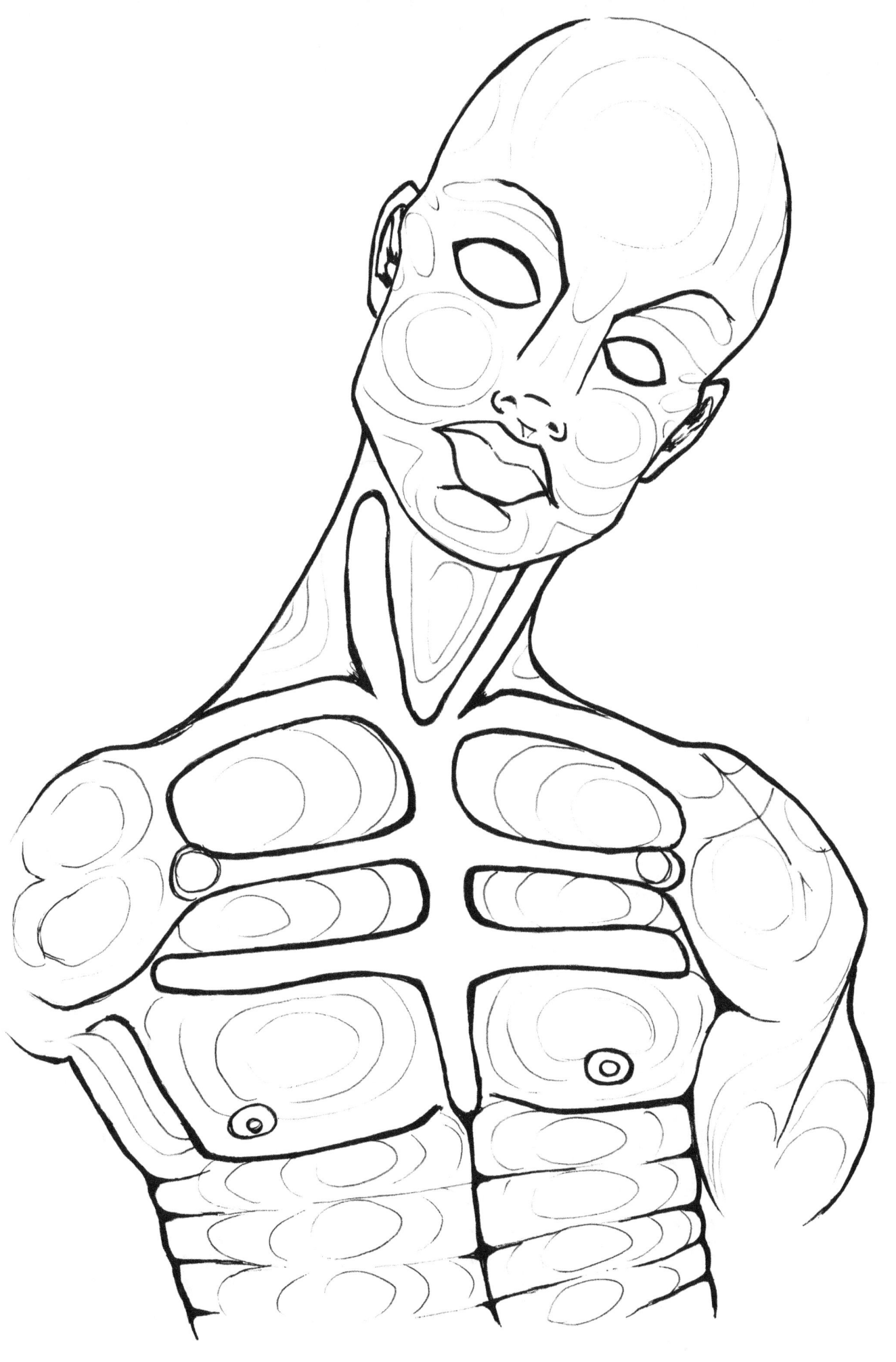

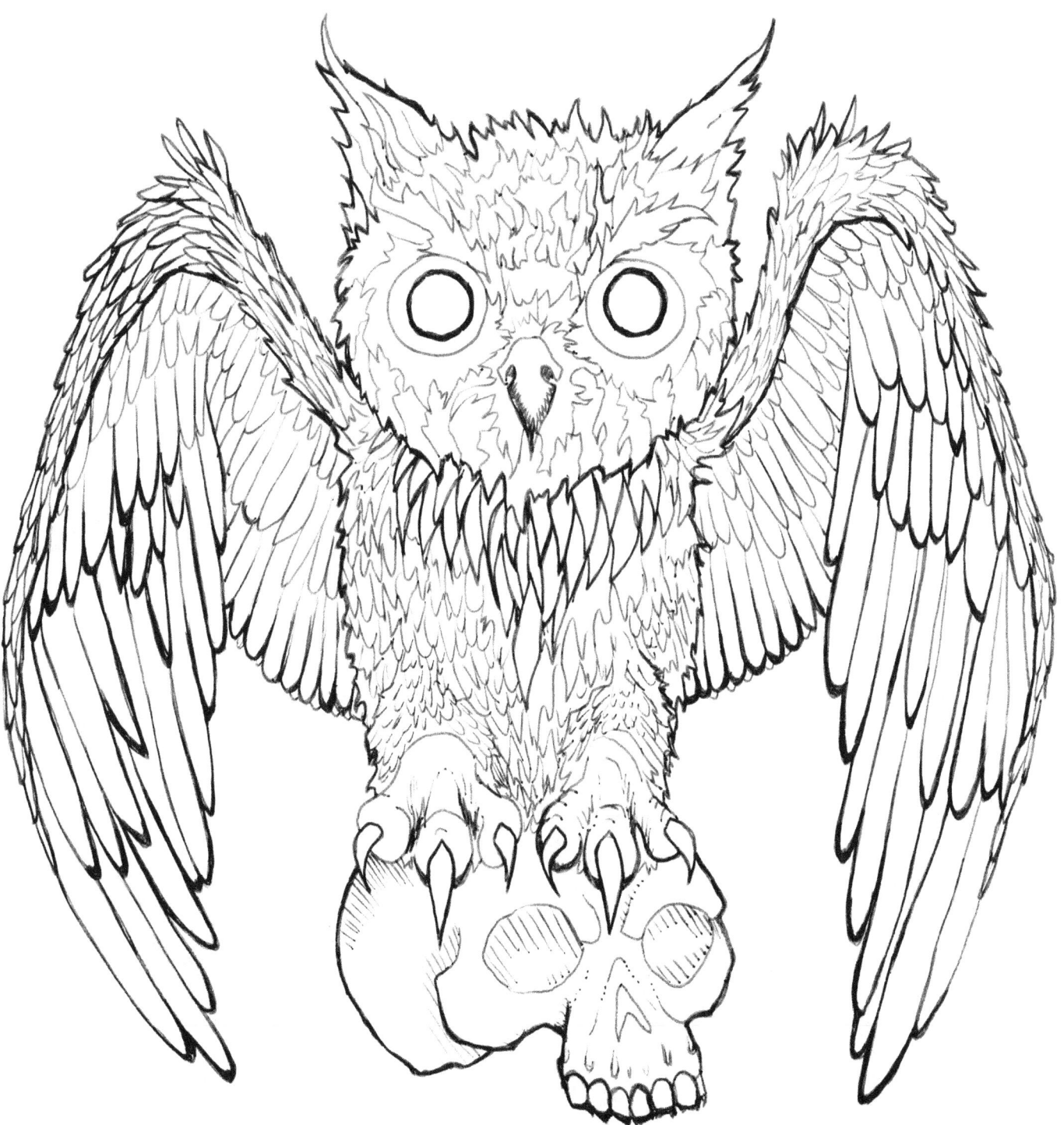

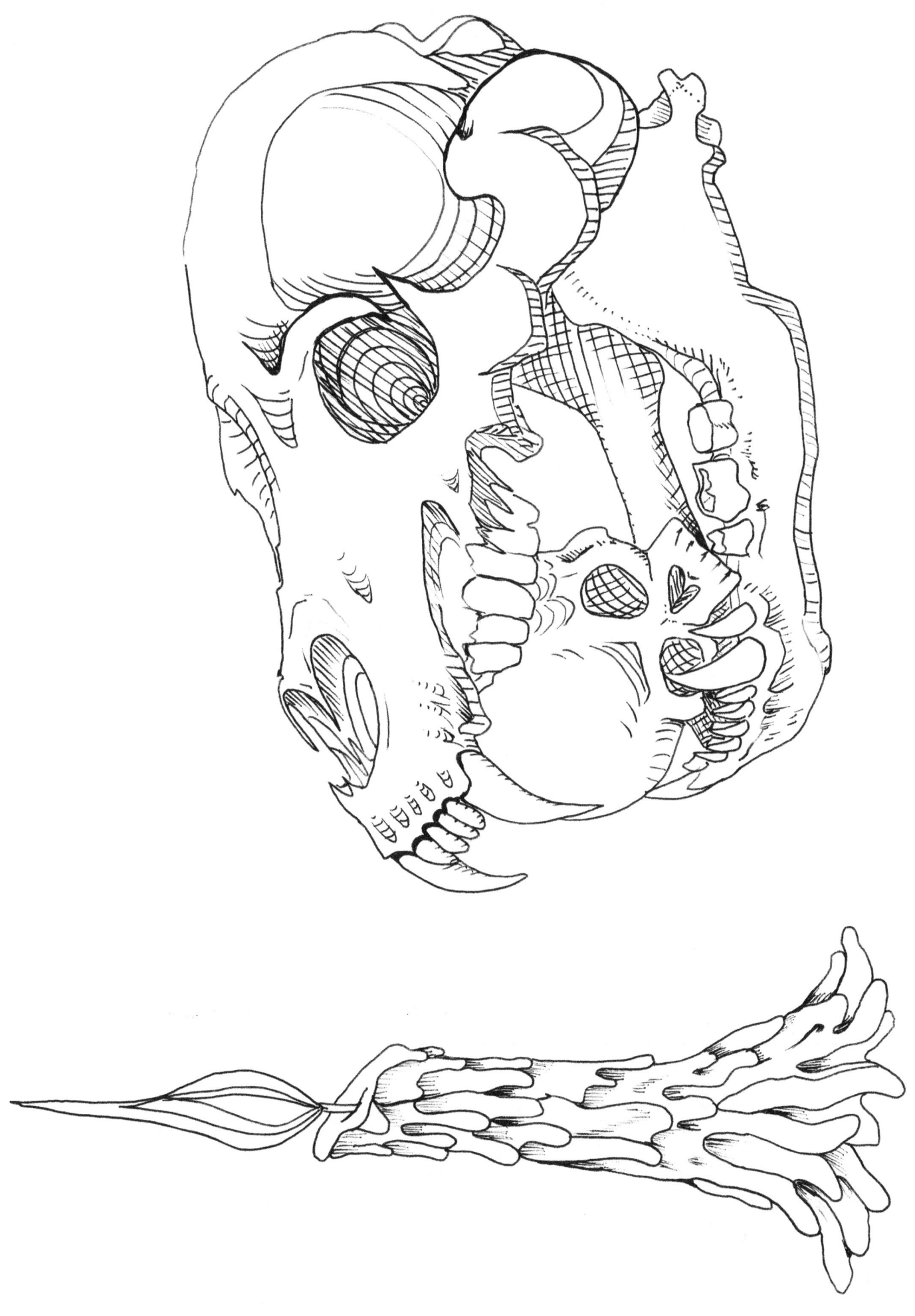

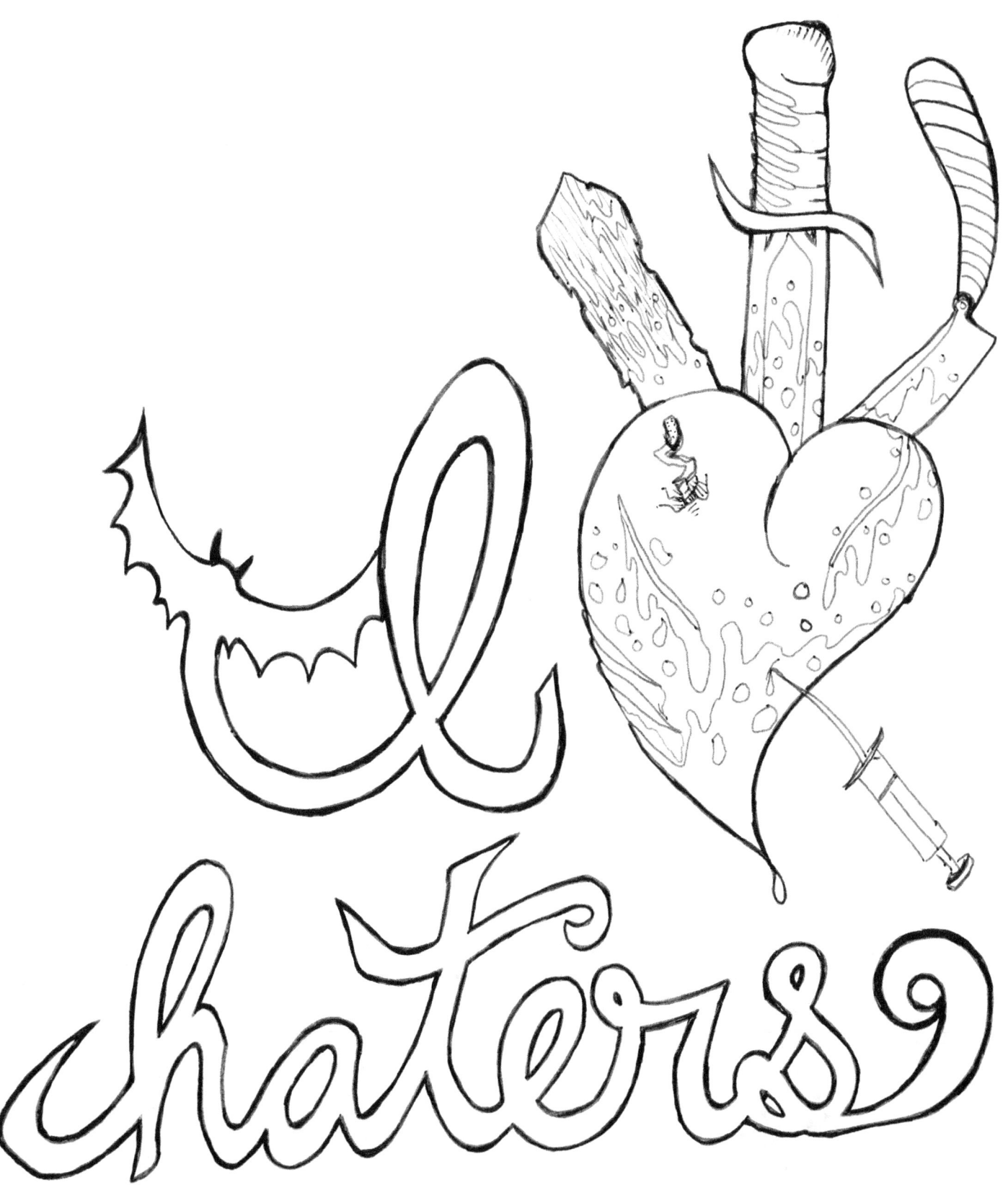

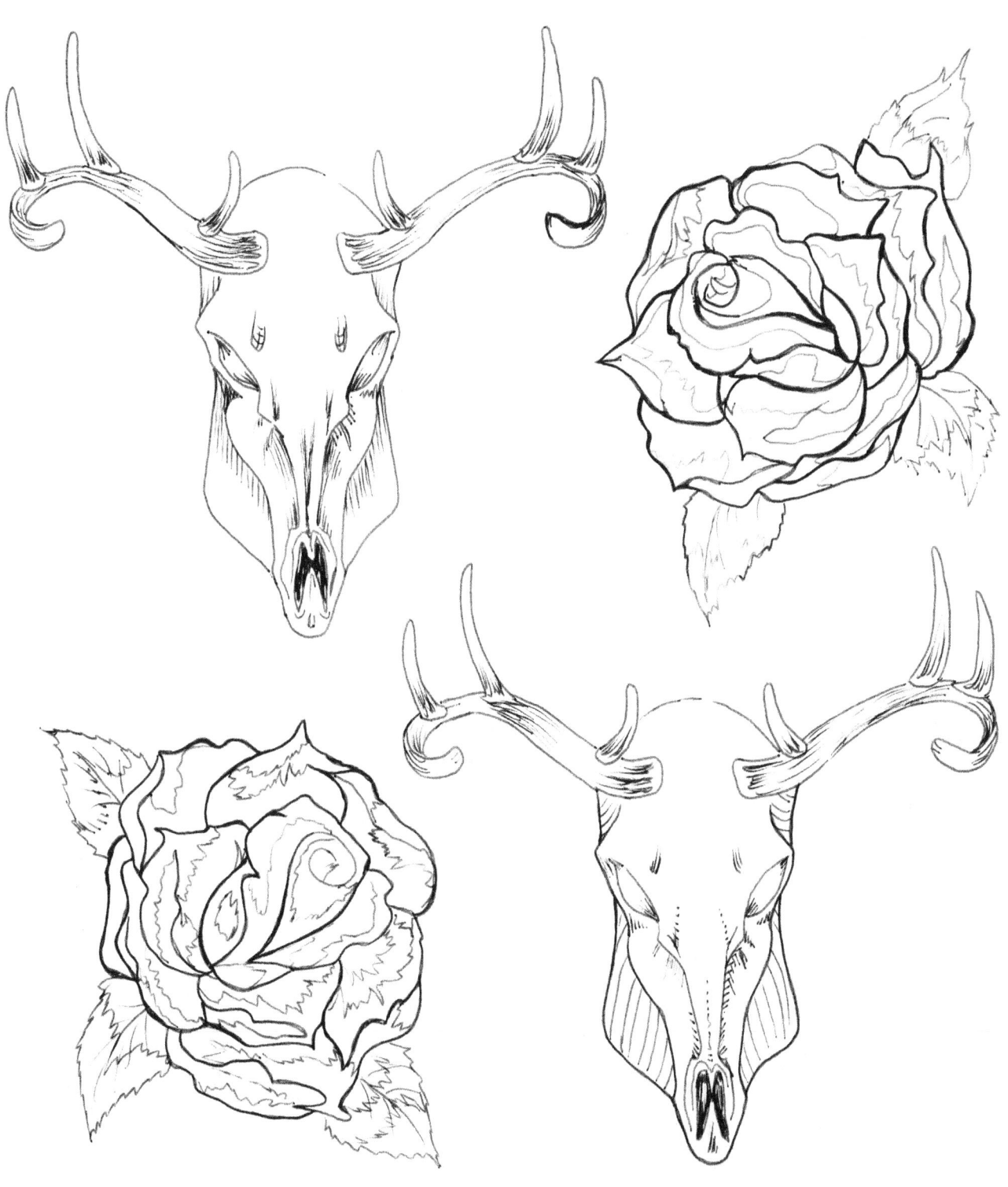

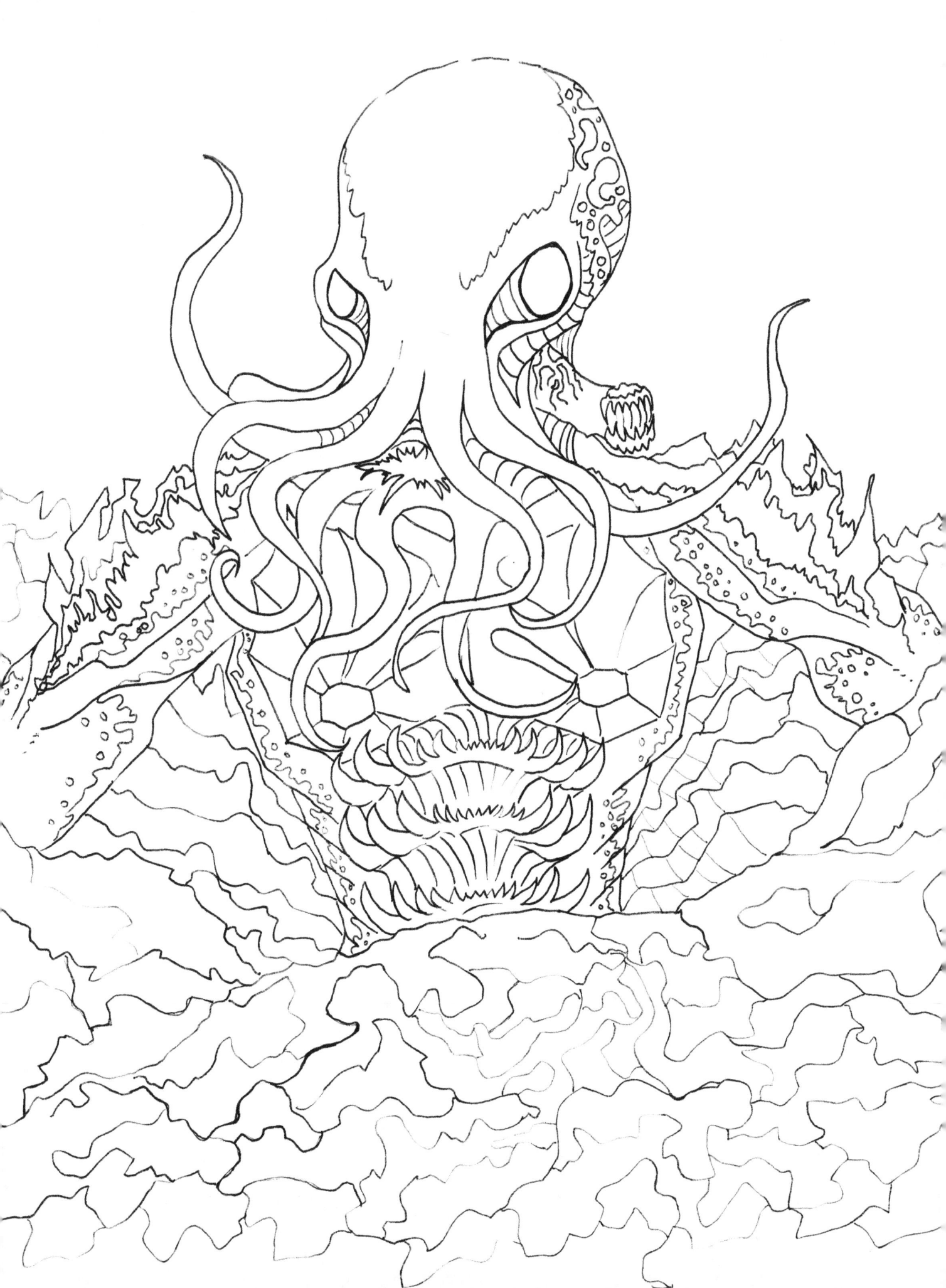

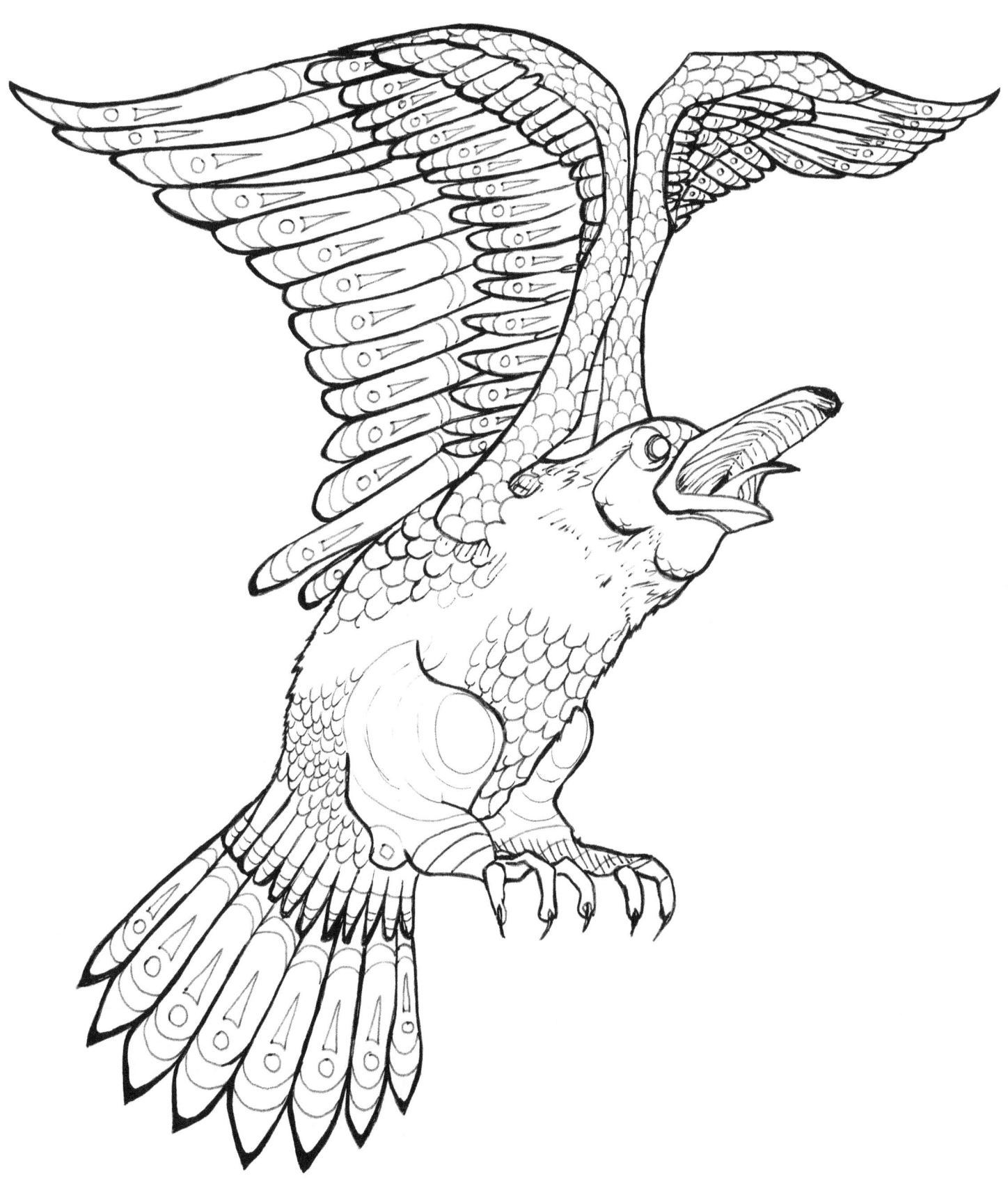

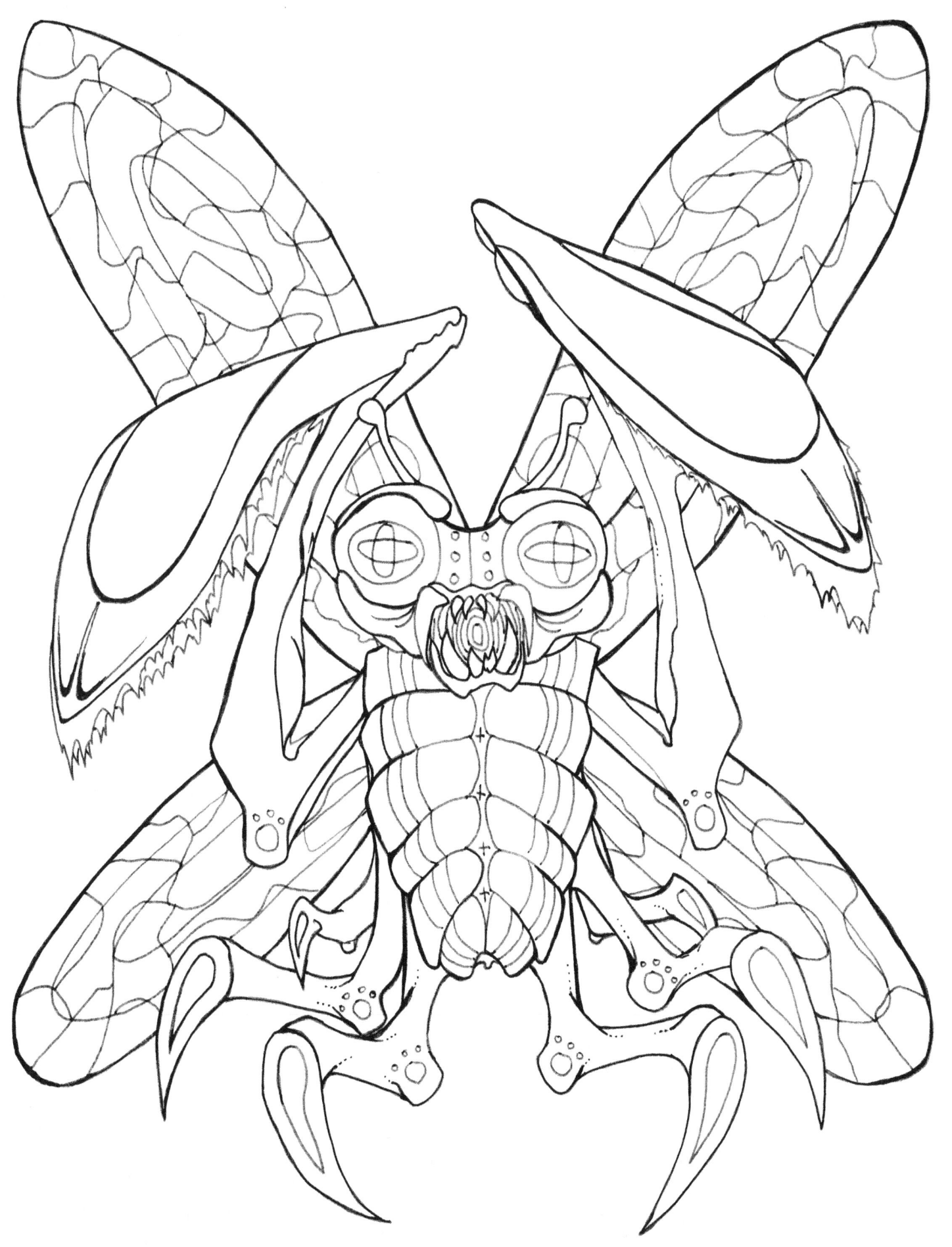

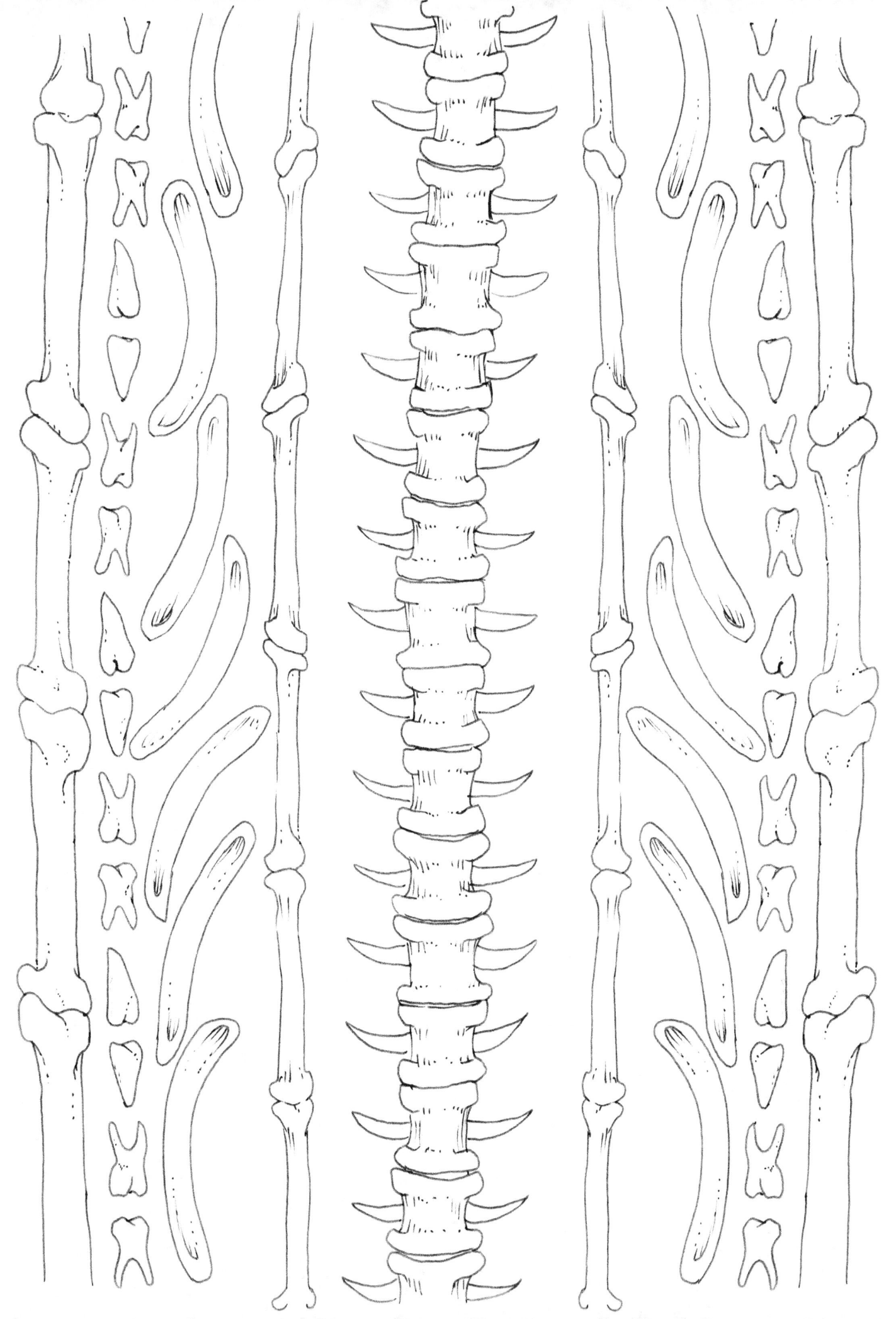

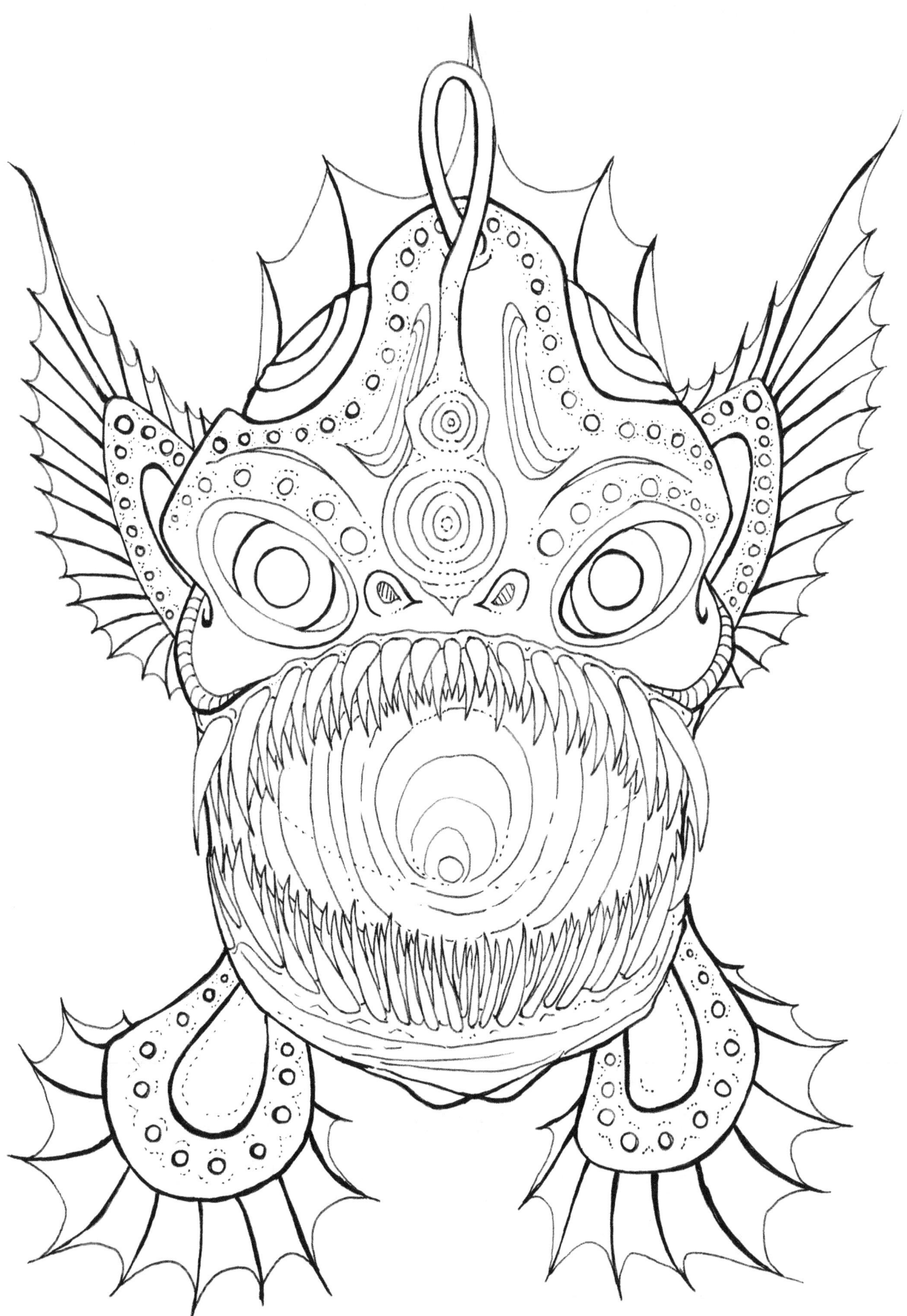

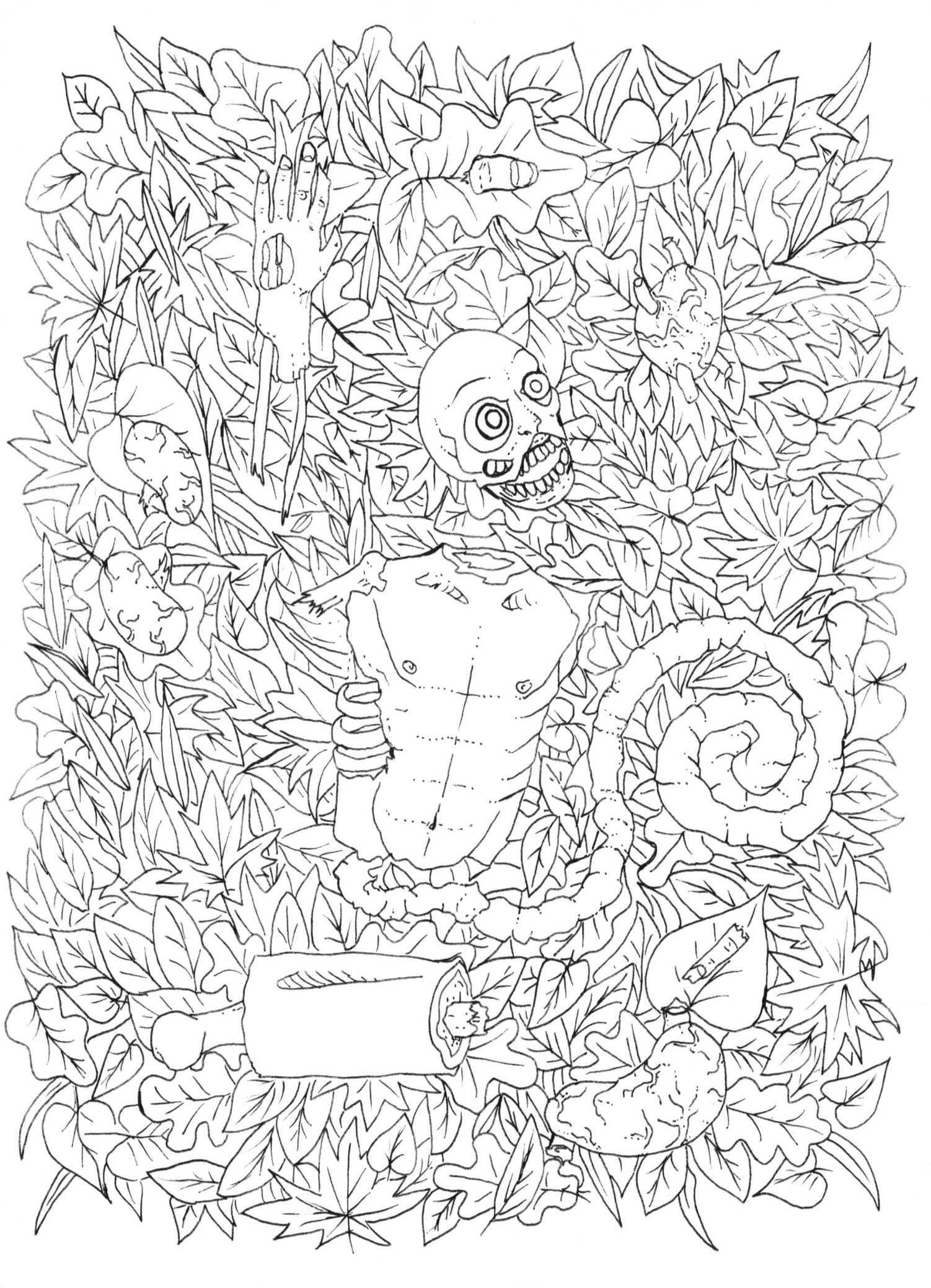

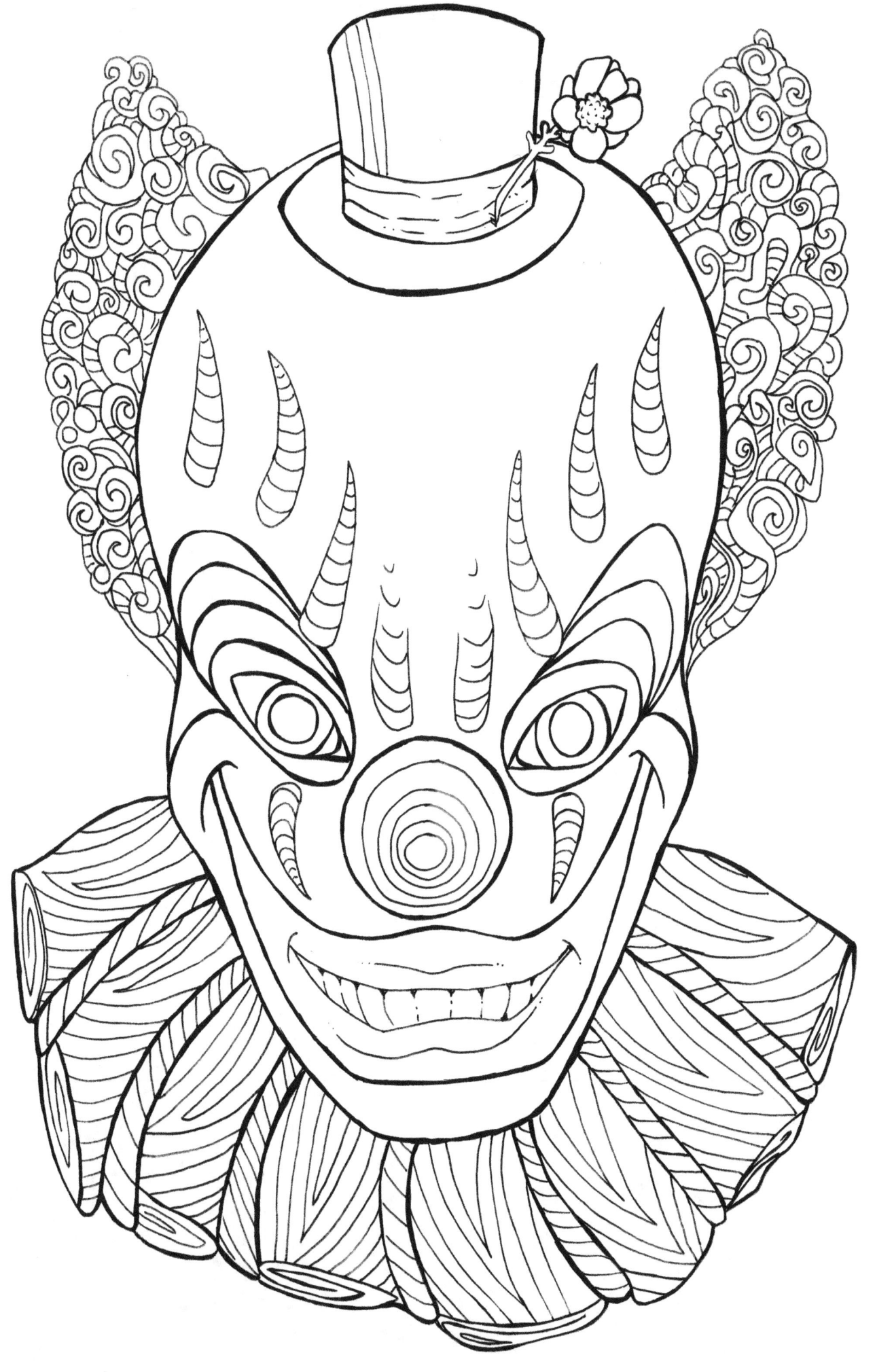

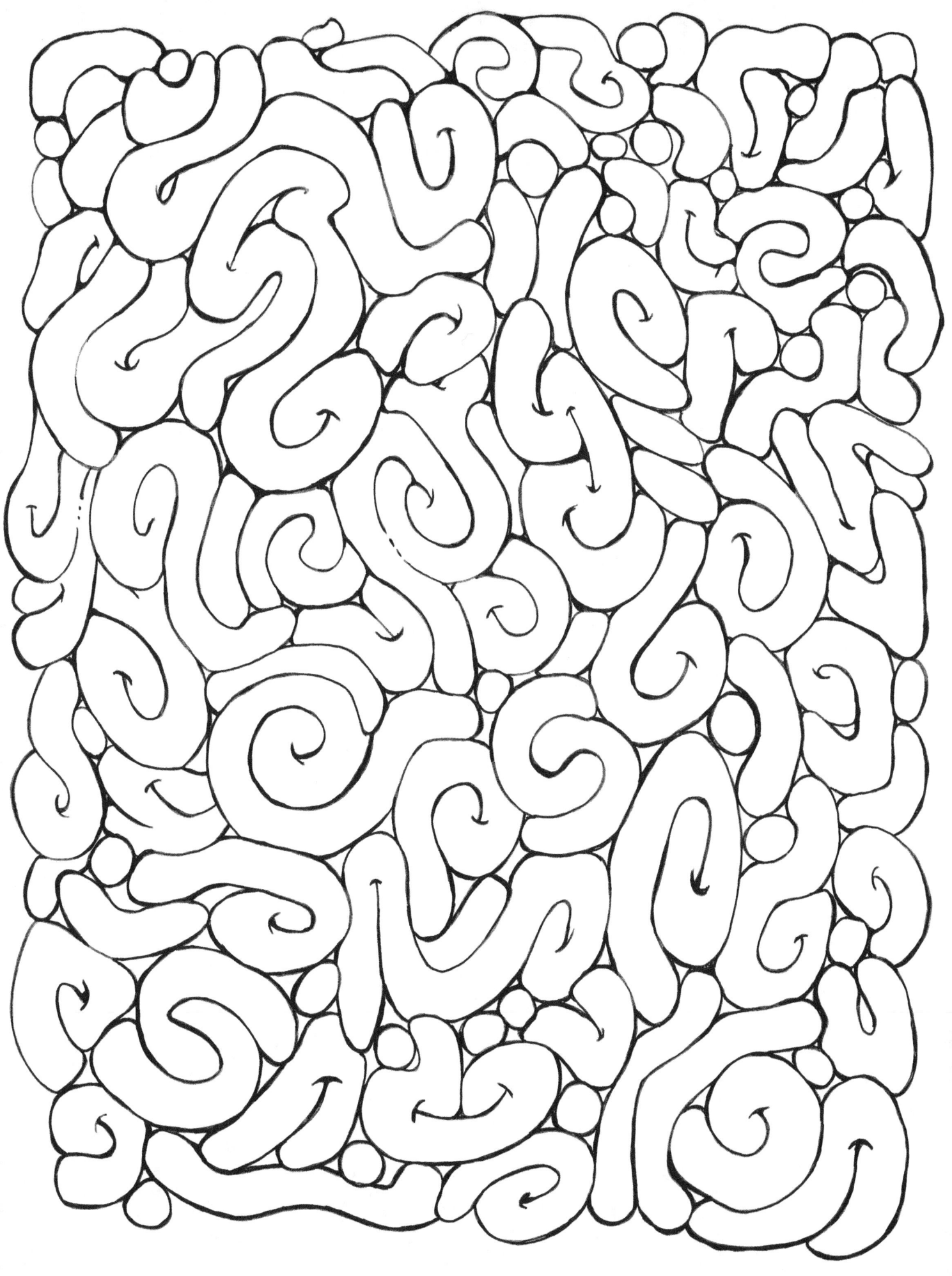

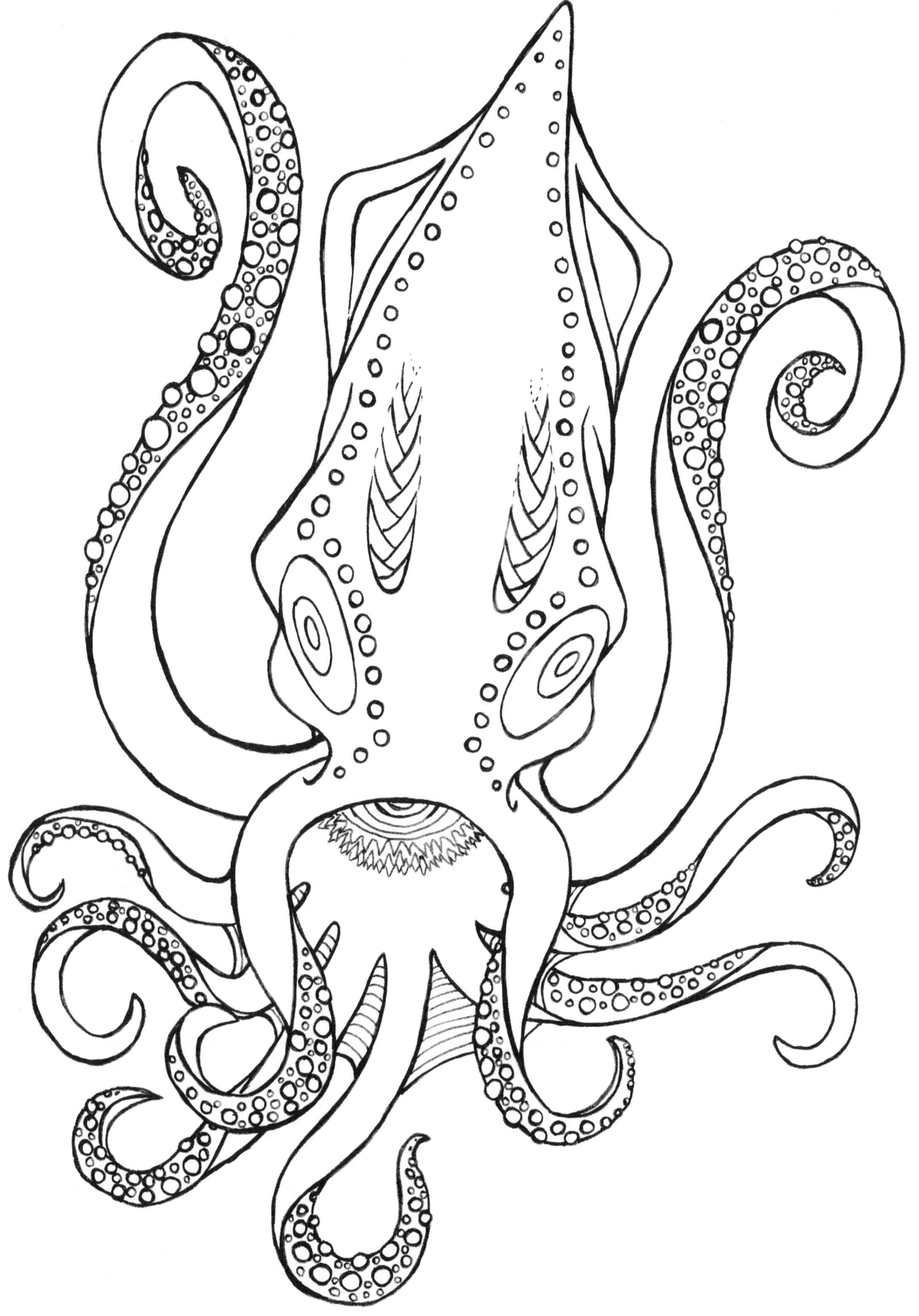

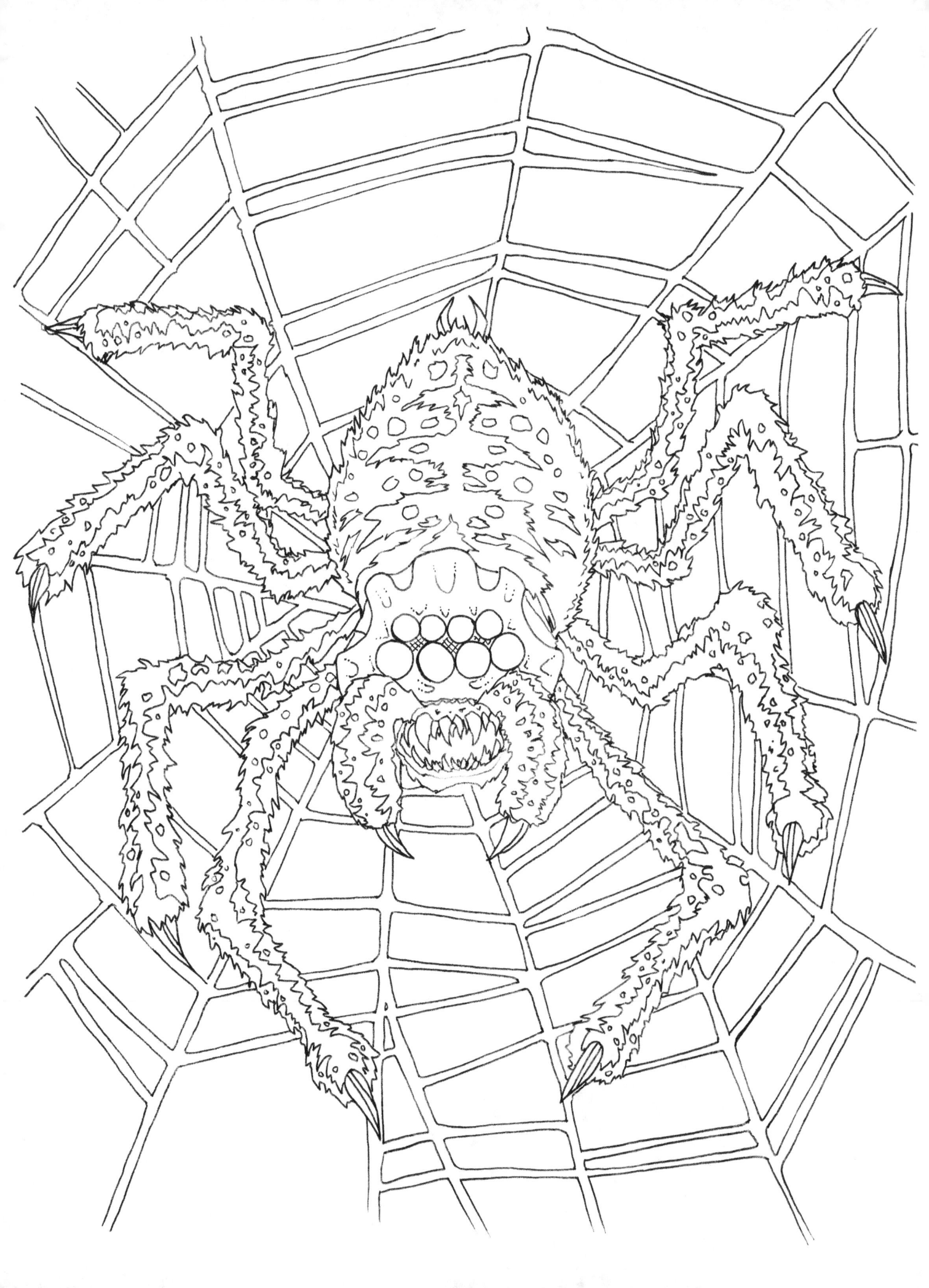

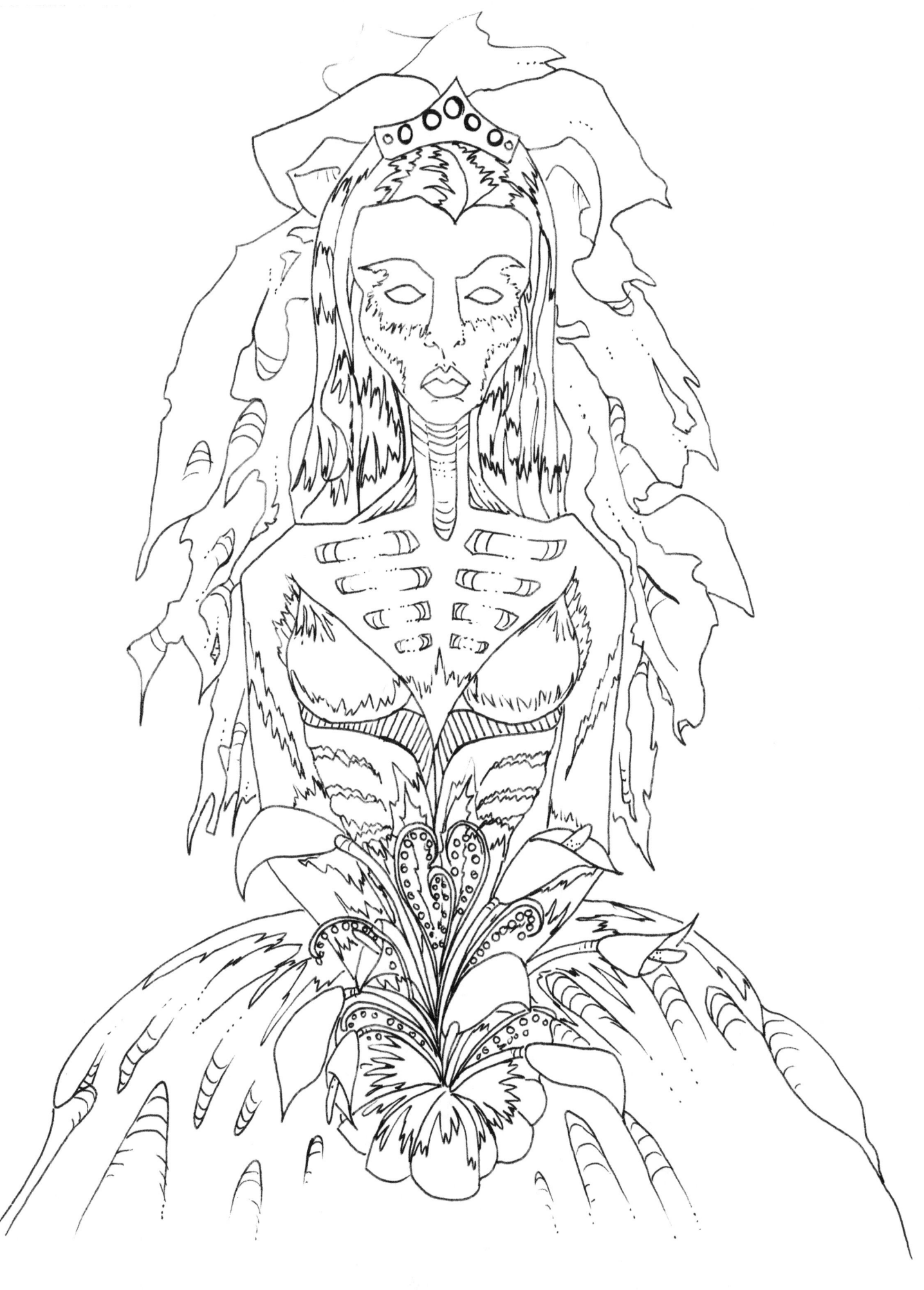

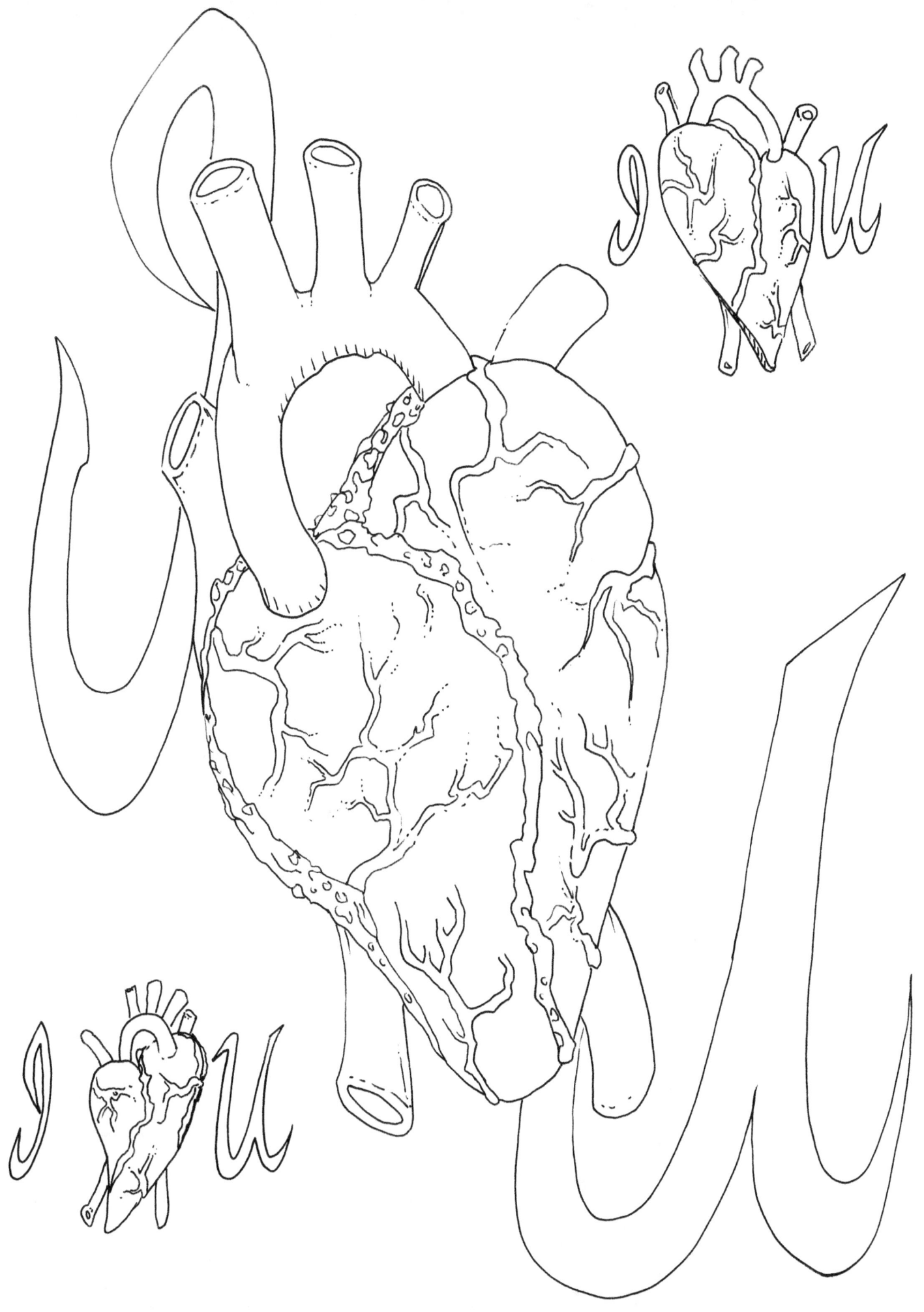

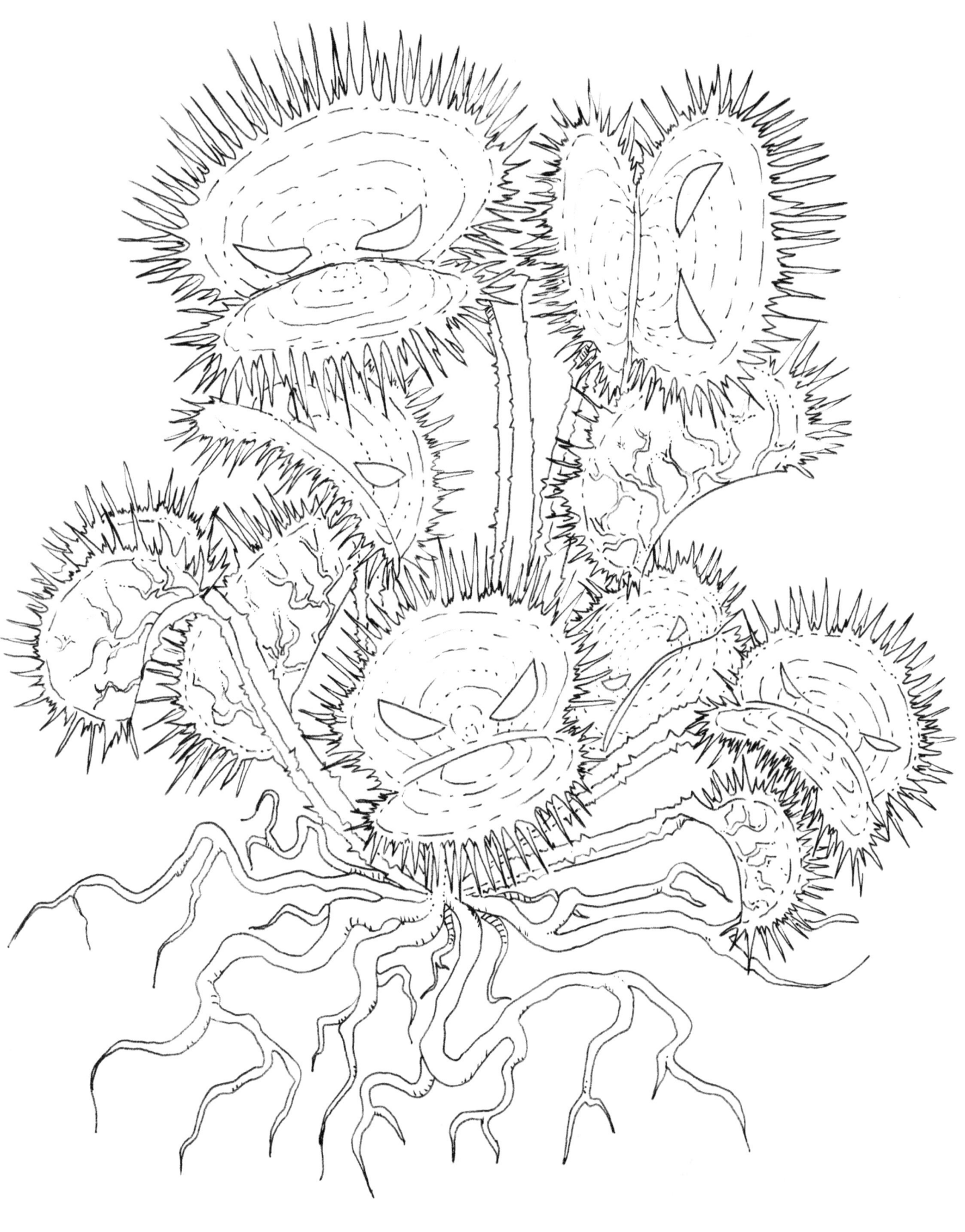

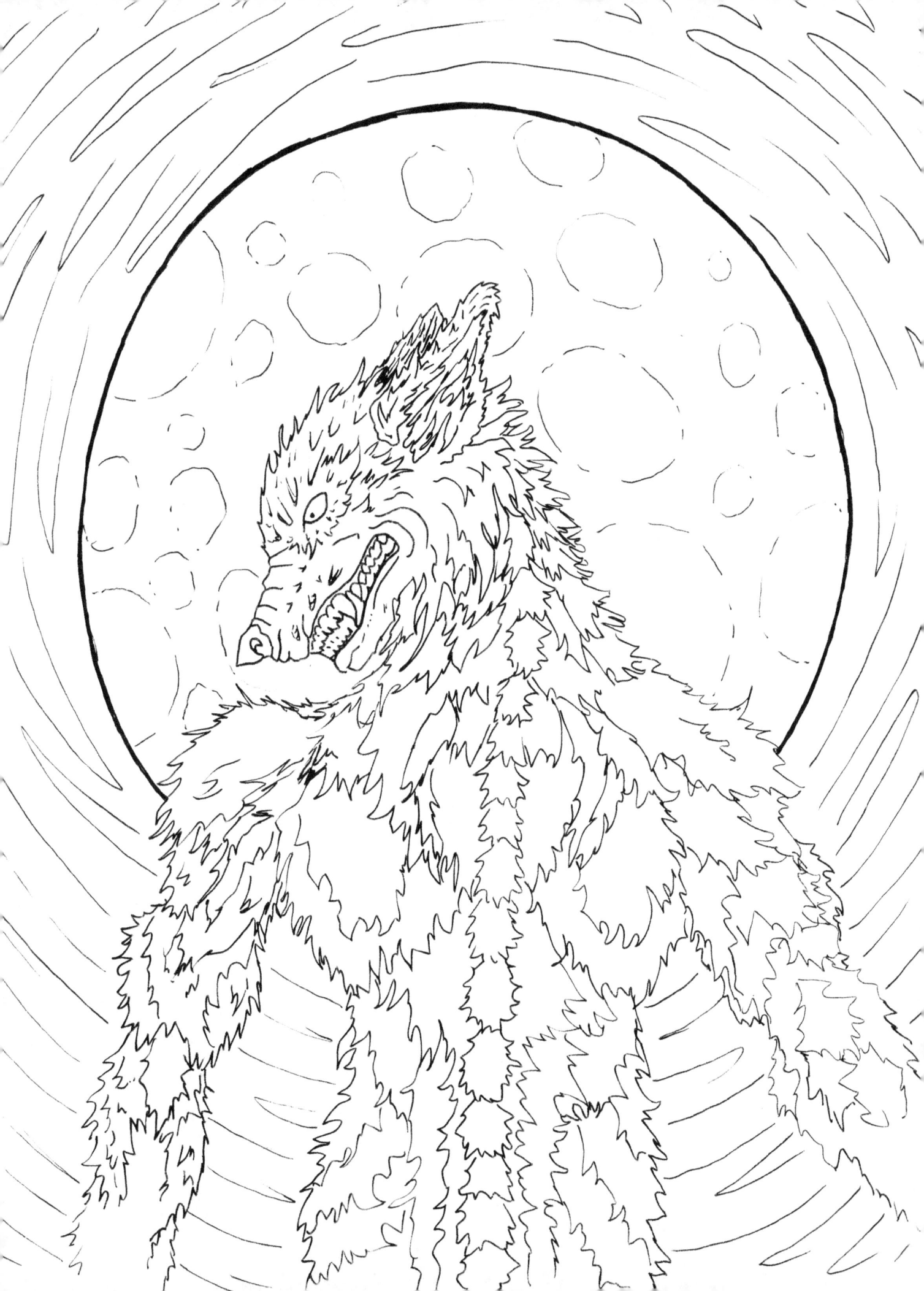

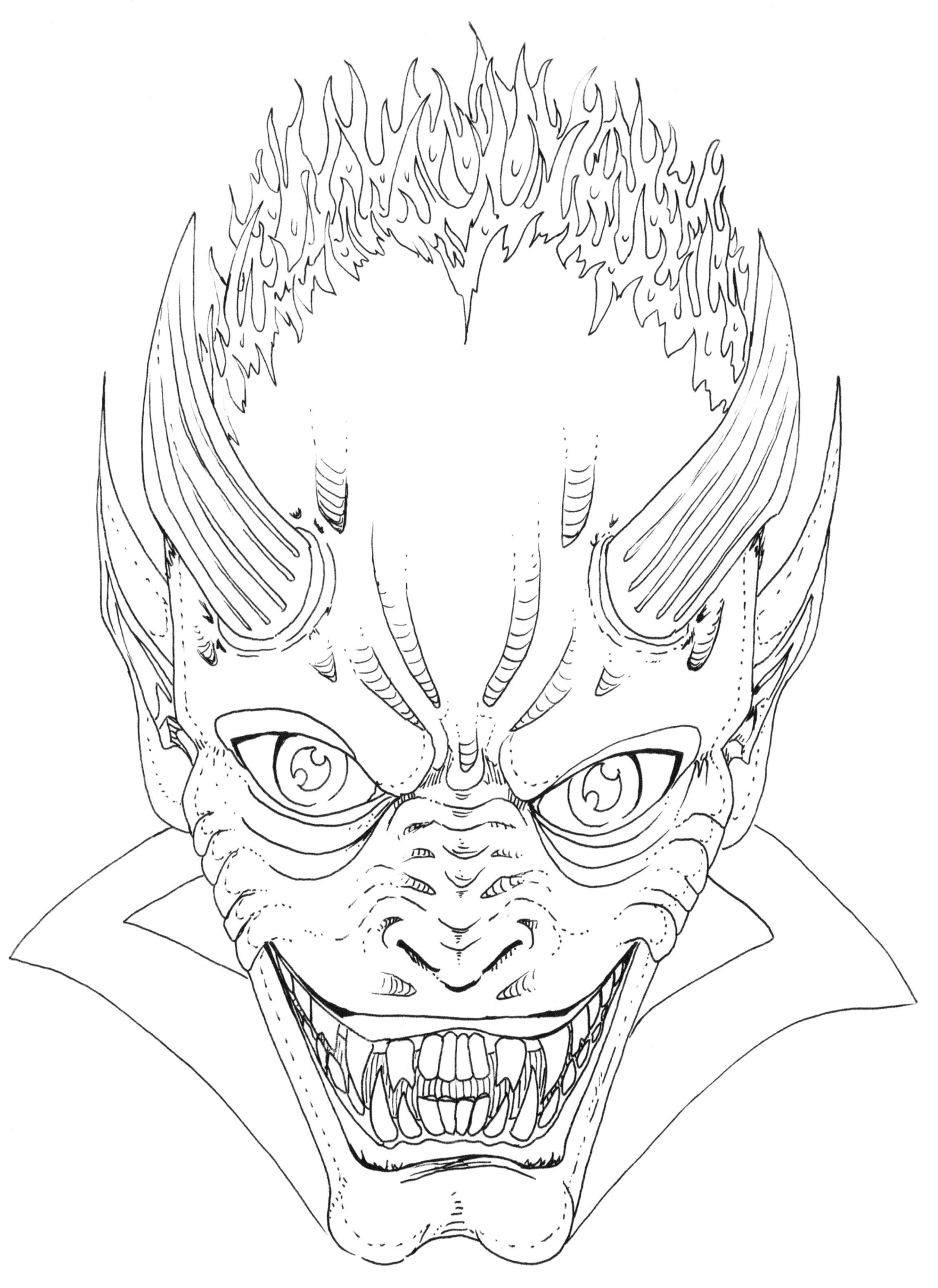

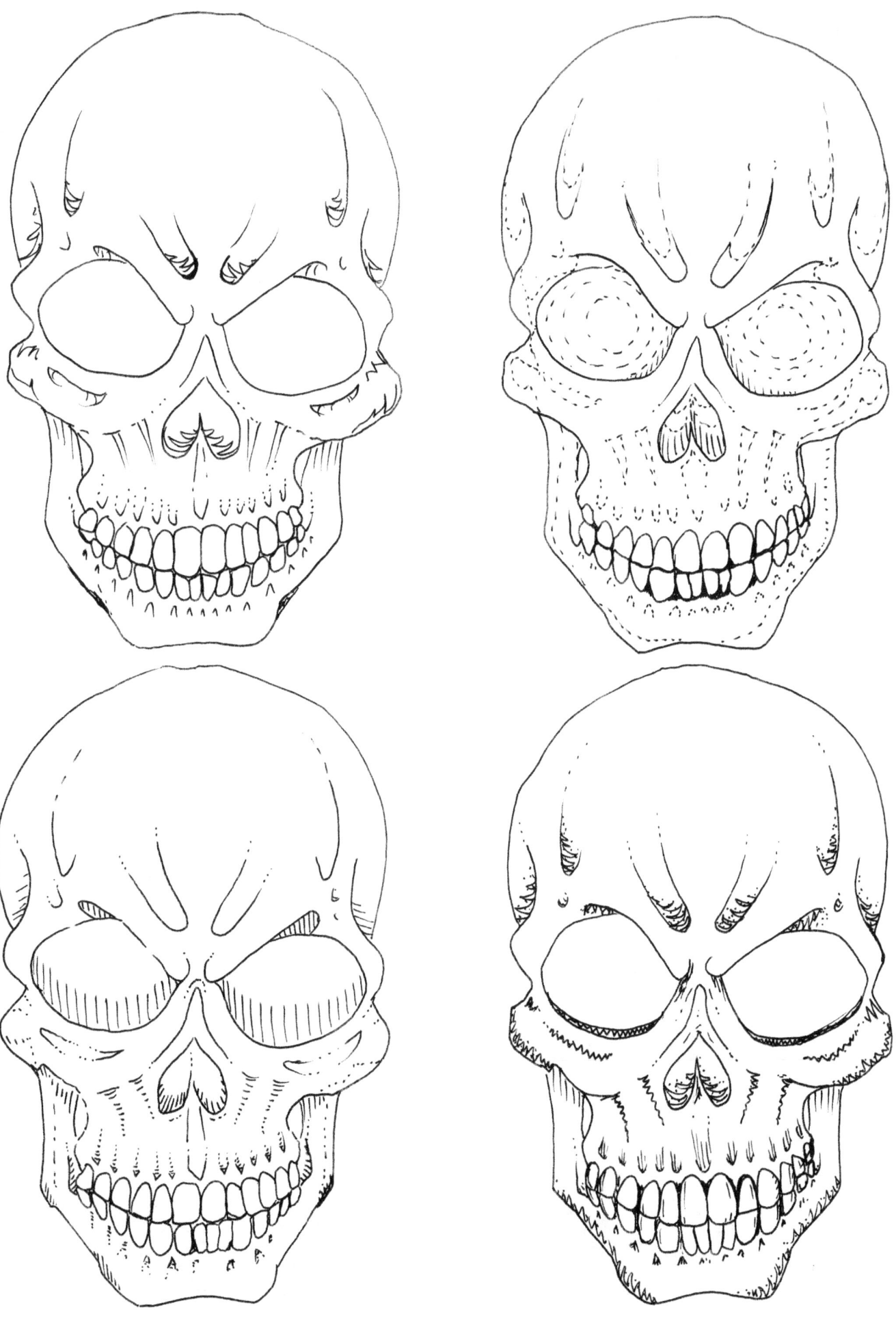

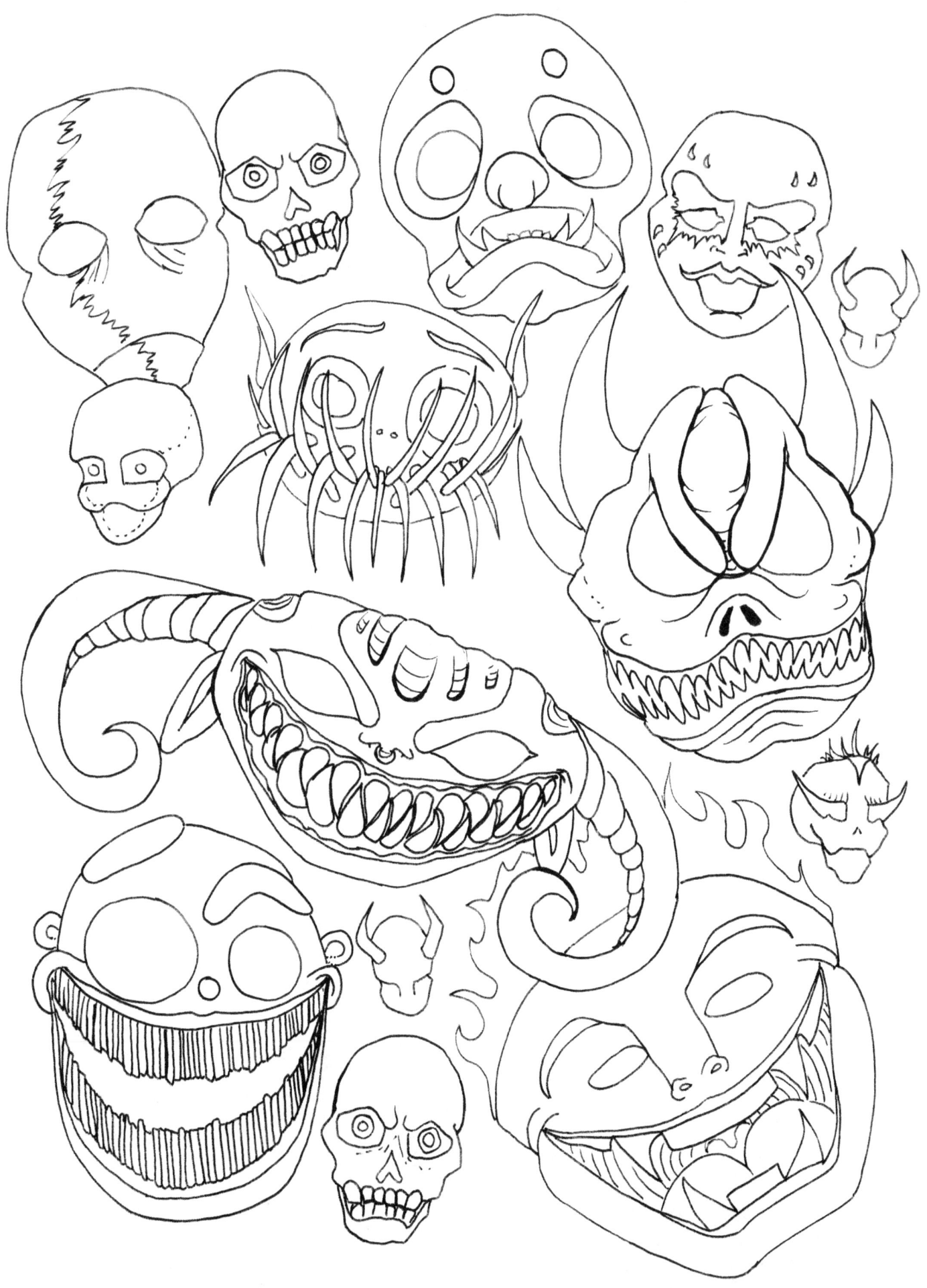

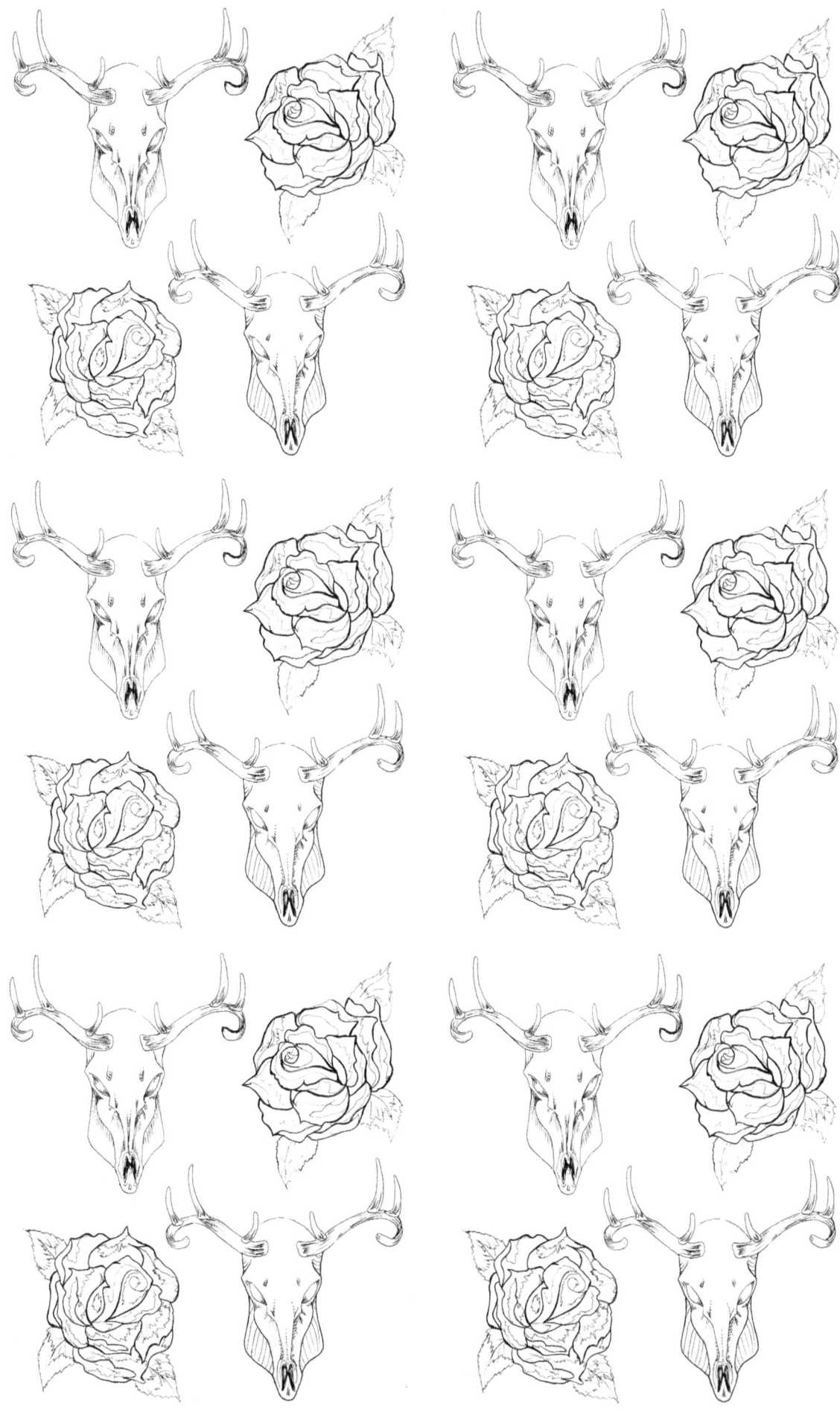

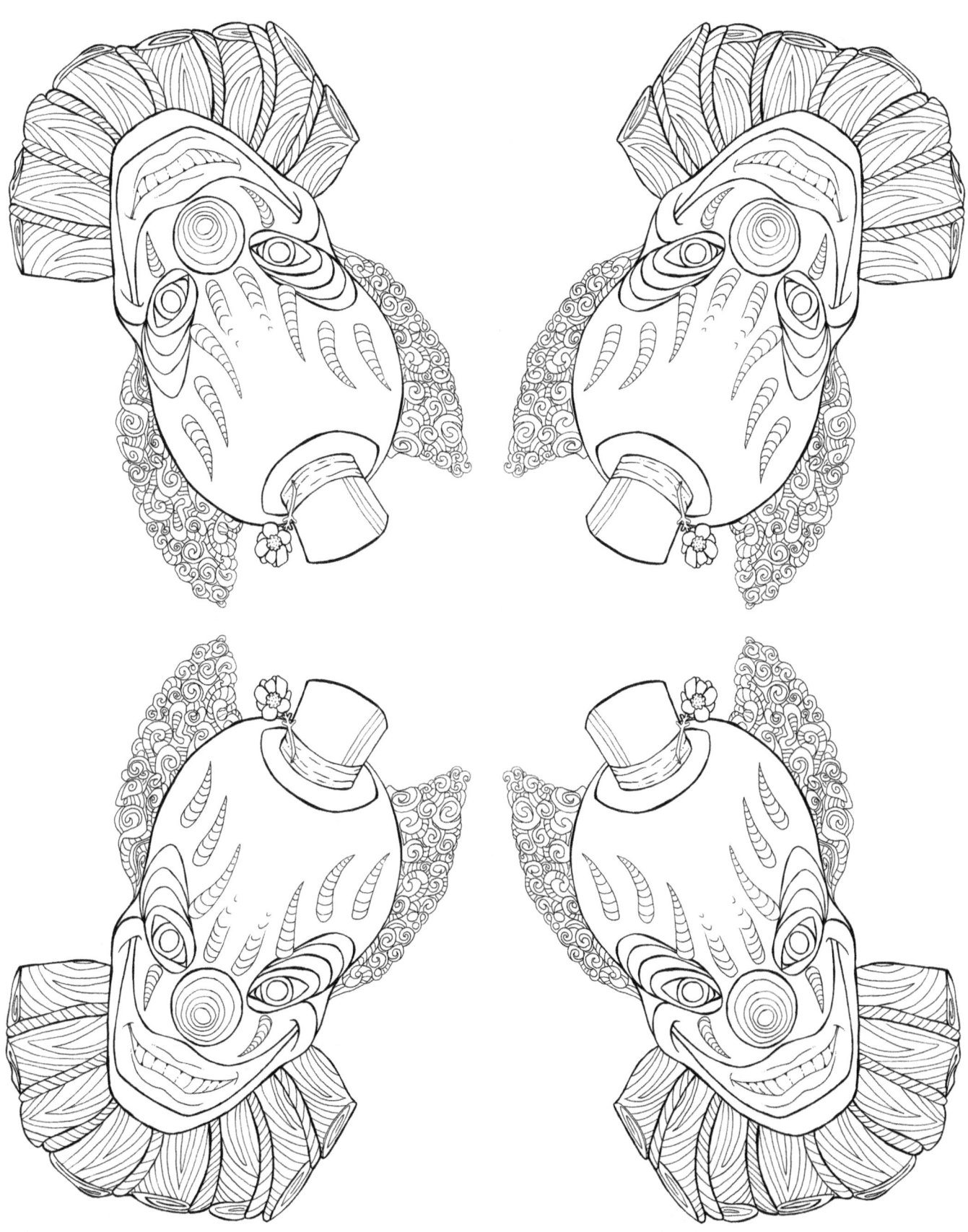